YOUR FUTURE IN
TECHNICAL AND SCIENCE WRITING

ARCO-ROSEN
CAREER GUIDANCE SERIES

# YOUR FUTURE IN
# TECHNICAL AND SCIENCE WRITING

Emerson Clarke & Vernon Root

arco
New York

Revised Edition
First Arco Printing, 1976

Published by Arco Publishing Company, Inc.
219 Park Avenue South, New York, N.Y. 10003
by arrangement with Richards Rosen Press, Inc.

Library of Congress Catalog Card Number 75-29659
ISBN 0-668-03914-0

Printed in the United States of America

VERNON M. ROOT                    EMERSON CLARKE

## *About the Authors*

RALPH E. CLARKE, who writes under the name *Emerson Clarke,* has had twenty years of experience in all aspects of technical and science writing. Since 1960, he has been manager of the technical services department of the special products division, Zenith Radio Corporation.

He has written three books previous to this one. His first, *A Guide to Technical Literature Production,* might almost be considered a predecessor to *Your Future in Technical and Science Writing,* since it covers the status of many of the same topics in the 1960's. His second book tells how to write proposals for government contracts, and his third is another guidebook, this one on the subject of aerospace-defense. In addition, Mr. Clarke has written extensively on writing, management, and information handling.

Mr. Clarke resides in River Forest, Illinois, with his wife, Marguerite, and four children.

VERNON M. ROOT, who was educated at Haverford and Yale, has

had two years' experience as a university professor in addition to eighteen years of technical publications experience and about fifteen years of active professional-society life.

He has spent his technical communication career at the Applied Physics Laboratory of The Johns Hopkins University, first as a technical editor, then as supervisor of education and training, and currently as supervisor of the technical reports group. A longtime Senior Member and Fellow of the Society of Technical Writers and Publishers (now the Society for Technical Communication), he has served as that organization's vice-president, two terms as its president, and for the last several years has headed its intersociety relations effort.

As a part of that effort, he worked for the formation of the new Council of Communication Societies, and served as its first president. The Council has issued a Directory of Communication Organizations that is a first in the communication profession. Dr. Root served as its compiler and editor.

Dr. Root lives in the Maryland suburbs of Washington, D.C., with his wife, Elspeth, and two children.

Dedicated to—
   Christine,
   Ralph,
   Suzanne, and
   Alison Clarke
and
   Christopher and
   Carolyn Root

# Contents

# Preface

Up to this point in your life, the road you have traveled has been fairly straightforward, with few turnoffs available to you. But now you have come to a place in the road where there are many branches, and you must choose among many possible ways.

You must select a career. The choice will commit you to a lifetime of endeavor in a specific area of human activity. Will that decision bring you both personal satisfaction and an adequate financial reward, or will it bring you perpetual frustration and small return for your lifetime of effort?

An important decision, indeed!

Your keenest need now is for facts. What lies down this road—is it for me? Or that road—what lies down there?

This book describes a road that many have stumbled upon in recent years and found uniquely satisfying, though few have set out to tread this path. It describes a career that is far less well known than physics, chemistry, engineering, biology, or medicine, but one that, in its own way, is no less satisfying or rewarding than those. It describes a career that combines the art of writing with the arts of science or technology or medicine. The facts about this career, its advantages and disadvantages, its rewards and tribulations, and the vast variety available within it, are covered in the chapters that follow.

Here, then, is the road that bears the signpost: *technical and science writing.*

Emerson Clarke
Vernon Root

## *In Grateful Acknowledgment*

This book has many authors in addition to the two names listed on the cover. The fields of technical writing and science writing are so broad and diverse that the authors sought help from a wide circle of associates. Their contributions will be found throughout the book in the form of comments on the profession in which they have achieved recognition. For this, our thanks, one and all.

Also, for good advice and guidance, the authors wish to thank Dr. Charles G. Roland of the Mayo Clinic and the American Medical Writers Association, Professor Joseph A. Rice of the University of Houston, Celima L. Hazard of the U.S. Civil Service Commission, and Henry L. Goodman of the Council for the Advancement of Science Writing.

# CHAPTER I

## Your Future in This Expanding Field

A great revolution is going on in this country and all over the world. It is not a new revolution. It began about three hundred years ago and has been picking up momentum ever since. It is a quiet revolution, not marked by violence or the overthrow of governments. Nevertheless, it is a revolution that has profoundly changed the lives of men in the past, and that will continue to change men's lives in unpredictable ways in the decades to come.

It is the revolution in our ways of living and our ways of thinking that has been brought about by the increasingly rapid growth of science and technology.

One of the most remarkable things about this revolution is the momentum it has picked up in recent years, as shown by two facts:

- Ninety percent of all scientists who have ever lived are alive today.
- In the decade of the 1960's, the amount of technical and scientific knowledge doubled; in the 1970's and beyond, it will multiply not two times, but three or four times.

At the beginning of the 1960's few questioned the value of science and technology or viewed their unfettered growth as anything but a boon to civilization. Now we are beginning to have second thoughts. The momentum gained by technology in the 1960's is beginning to look like a spinning flywheel that is being spun faster, ever faster. We are beginning to be seriously concerned that, unless that momentum is brought rapidly under some controls, our civilization, like the flywheel, may soon exceed its cohesive limits and fly to pieces.

The evidence of our plight is mounting and worrisome. The products of our modern technology—from our higher live-birth rates and dropping death rates to our undisposable, nonreturnable cans and bottles to our noxious auto and industrial exhausts—are almost out of control; unless we can learn to control them, they can destroy us. Choking clouds blanket our cities; crowds of people choke the cities' streets; rivers once pure enough to drink from are channels for all manner of industrial wastes; and refuse is being generated so quickly that it could fill the Grand Canyon to the brim by the year 2000!

Although the blame for many of our ecological problems lies with our use of modern technology, only through more perceptive use of science and technology have we any hope of solving them.

But to do so, our scientists and engineers need the support of a skeptical public. As scientists have gone about the business of seeking new knowledge and creating new developments, a widening gap—a communication gap—has opened between them and society. Equally serious are the communication gaps among the scientists and engineers themselves. As a result, there is a vital need for people with special skills to help bridge those gaps. The primary "bridgers" are *technical and science writers*.

At first glance, it might seem that the technical writer writes about the technology—the tangible hardware that results from engineering development, whereas the science writer writes about science— biology, chemistry, physics, and so forth. But that is not the way those terms are used—the profession distinguishes between technical and science writers in terms of their audiences.

- Technical writing is writing about engineering and science for a *technically trained* audience.
- Science writing is writing about engineering and science for a *general* audience, usually the general public.

Although the two fields sometimes approach each other rather closely, they are really quite distinct. Technical writers work primarily on technical reports or manuals that are sent to a relatively small group (usually fewer than five hundred) of other scientists or engineers who are working in the same general area, or to a small group of technicians who are going to use and maintain a specific piece of equipment. Science writers, on the other hand, work mostly for large-city daily newspapers or for major news magazines. They write articles about scientific, medical, space, and technological developments for a readership that numbers at least in the hundreds of thousands. As we will see, those vastly different audiences require distinctly different approaches to writing.

Occasionally, however, the two fields do approach each other. The technical writer will be asked to prepare a brochure to help sell a particular product or tell his organization's technical history. Although such booklets are not for the general public, their audience is not so narrow as that of a manual. Similarly, the science writer may collaborate on an article for a magazine such as *Scientific American* in which his audience is both smaller and more scientifically sophisticated than his usual one.

In another sense, too, technical and science writing are alike in more than their subject matter. They share a common objective, namely, to provide the reader with clear, accurate, precise, unbiased information on the basis of which he can make informed decisions.

## Rewards of the Profession

Well, that is a capsule comparison of the two professions we are talking about. But why should anyone want to enter them? Because they are fun; they are important; they are interesting, challenging, and diverse in their opportunities; and they pay reasonably well.

*Fun.* For the right person—the person who likes to work with words (and who likes to make words work for *him*) and who knows about and is interested in science—putting science stories into words is fun. For some people the fun is in making the story so explicit and precise that technicians will have no trouble following it. For others, the fun is in explaining a new development so that its significance will be clear to management. For a few, the fun is in bringing scientific developments to life so that they catch the imagination of the general public.

*Important Contribution.* But beyond the fun of his job, the writer contributes to progress. When men first began to devise useful technological machines, they were not being pressed by scheduled deadlines. Leonardo da Vinci had time not only to paint and envision new devices (see Fig. 1), but also to serve as his own technical writer and illustrator. Today, the pressure of development schedules has made the work of the writer vitally important. Through his work, engineers and scientists can devote more attention to their research and development work. Through his ability to communicate quickly and effectively, the writer speeds up the interchange of information. If a technical writer, he may make a vital contribution to the deter-

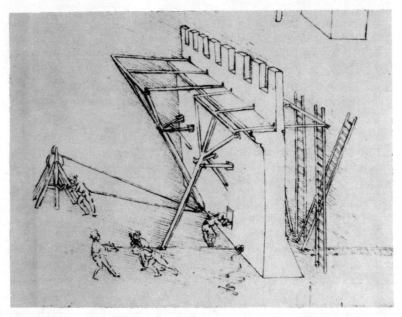

"Where the bombards should fail in their effect, I shall make catapults, ballistas, blunderbusses, and other engines of marvelous efficacy, unknown to customary practice; and, in general, to suit the manifold variety of occasions, I shall construct all sorts of different things for purposes of attack and defense."

*Fig. 1. The work of an early technical and science writer (and illustrator!), Leonardo da Vinci (1483). The illustration is from Leonardo's* Codex Atlanticus *(Hoepli Publisher, Milan, Italy); the text is from Antonina Vallentin's* Leonardo da Vinci: The Tragic Pursuit of Perfection, *translated by E. W. Dickes (New York: The Viking Press, 1938).*

rence of world conflict; if a science writer, he may make a vital contribution to the survival of the planet.

*Interesting Work.* There is almost no limit to the number of interesting assignments a qualified writer can receive. Writers have supported and reported the nation's space programs, from its weather, communication, and navigation satellites to its Herculean effort to place man's footsteps on the moon. Writers have supported and reported the nation's effort to maintain a posture of military deterrence, from the successful Polaris submarines to the ill-fated F-111 swing-wing fighter-bomber. Writers have supported and reported the nation's atomic energy program, from the excitement of the first self-sustaining chain reaction to the development of nuclear power plants. In the future, writers will document and describe the nation's battle to control pollution, its struggle to save the cities, and its search for alternative transportation systems. They will continue to report man's fight against disease and disability. Where the action is, there the writer is.

*Challenge.* The profession—whether of science writing or technical writing—offers a clear challenge. Words serve man well, but they can be his worst enemy. Words can twist and tangle themselves into unintelligible jumbles. The writer and editor must seek out the true meanings and set the facts down clearly and simply. Often the engineer is so close to the work he is doing that he finds it difficult to stand back and evaluate it with an outsider's critical eye. Performing that evaluative function is part of the challenge of being a technical or science writer. By helping the engineer to see both his work and his words as others will see them, the writer can help him unsnarl word jumbles and convert them into clear, straight streams of prose.

*Entry into Engineering and Scientific Circles.* A man without an advanced academic degree usually cannot work in the higher echelons of research and development. As a technical and science writer, however, his special skills make him a welcome partner in such circles.

*Diversity of Experience.* Writers and editors always cover a broader spectrum of scientific or technical knowledge than do the engineers or scientists with whom they work. The engineer, scientist, or physician is an expert in one specialty; the writer lacks this technical expertise, but is able to write competently about a wide range of specialties. He knows enough of the phraseology and methodology of science or medicine to understand what a scientist or physician is trying to say even though in some cases it may not be said very well.

*Opportunity to Gain New Knowledge.* As a result of the diversity of specialties within which the writer must work, his opportunities to gain new knowledge are greater than those of the average researcher. To write effectively about each new area in which he is asked to work, the writer must have a basic understanding of that area. Thus, in each new assignment, the writer has an opportunity to explore a new field. Often he is given access to a considerable body of new information on the subject that is not readily available to other people.

*Good Salary.* In the past decade, as writers have gained professional recognition, their salaries have increased sharply. As we turn into the 1970's, their salaries are at a relatively stable level just a bit below those of scientists and engineers, but on a par with other professional service groups such as personnel specialists. In the future, we can expect the salaries of writers and editors to remain close to those of scientists and engineers.

## Your Career?

Is this career for you? It is an ideal career for those who can write well and who have a natural interest in some aspects of science, but whose inclination is toward a broad, relatively shallow approach to science as opposed to an in-depth investigation of one small area.

## Keys to Success

What does it take to succeed in this career? There are four requirements: first, a natural interest backed by a formal education in things scientific, technical, or medical; second, an understanding of the methods and theories by which scientists and engineers or biological and medical researchers work; third, natural skill and interest in using the tools of communication, especially flexible, easy, accurate use of the English language; and fourth, a greater desire to write about science and technology, or biology and medicine, than to practice them. Add to those factors the well-known requisites that lead to success in almost any field, namely, initiative, the ability to get along well with other people, and dedication to accomplishing the task at hand, and the portrait of the successful technical or science writer is complete.

Surprisingly, you need not have an engineering degree to write for engineers (though it helps). Neither is an advanced degree in a science necessary to a science writer (though it helps, too). The prime requirement in either career is a sound foundation of scientific or engineering knowledge based on detailed training or formal education in some scientific or engineering discipline so that when the challenge of a new project comes along, you will be able to learn quickly, building upon what you already know.

## Your Future in the Profession

The potential of this career in writing is an exciting one. The span of time between now and the year 2000, a span that will cover the major part of your career, will be a time of unpredictably great achievement. All the pressing problems that threaten our nation and the world will have to be dealt with. New housing must be constructed on a scale never before attempted. Medical electronics equipment must be put to work to relieve the shortage of doctors and health facilities. New modes of transportation must be developed for use within and between our cities. Safe, effective, and culturally acceptable techniques must be devised to control our population growth. An avalanche of information must be processed and put to effective use. Most important of all, the environment must be restored to wholesomeness for the race to survive.

If our people will it, all those goals can be achieved with the help of science and technology. In that achievement, technical and science writers will be key participants.

CHAPTER II

## *Where You May Work*

Wherever there is science and technology, there is a story to be told of its progress and its achievements. And there, telling that story, you will find technical and science writers.

They work in industry, in business, in government, in research and development laboratories, in medical laboratories, in newspaper and magazine offices, and even in their own homes as free-lancers. They are found in every major city all across the country. As is to be expected, technical writers are more numerous where engineers and scientists are concentrated—in industries that rely upon research for new products (such as the aerospace, electronics, computer, and defense industries), in universities, and in government laboratories. Geographically, in the Far West, technical writers are most numerous in California and in Washington state; in the South, they are concentrated in Florida, Alabama, and Texas; in the East they are found mainly in Massachusetts, New York, and Maryland; and in the Mid-Central region, in Illinois, Ohio, and Minnesota.

Science writers are based primarily in major cities where they work for major daily newspapers and weekly or monthly news magazines.

*You May Write for Industry . . .*

### . . . *About Consumer and Industrial Products*
Along with his product, the manufacturer must provide an indispensable service. He must tell how to operate that product; he must tell how to maintain it; and, increasingly, he must tell how to put it

together. The more complex the product, the more extensive are the instructions that go with it. A power lawnmower for the homeowner requires a certain set of rather simple instructions for its operation and maintenance. A computer requires another set, but these instructions are much more complex. A child's wagon, swing set, or Christmas game probably needs to be assembled before it can be used; the required instructions are not as complicated as those for a computer— they only seem so to Dad at 2 A.M. on Christmas. And so it is for just about everything produced for the consumer by American industry: the dishwashers, television and radio sets, automobiles, and snowmobiles; and for the things produced for industry itself: the control systems, machine tools, business machines, and computers.

It is not just an added service, this supplying of instructions; it is an inseparable part of the product. If the customer cannot operate the product, or cannot maintain it (or have it maintained), he will consider the product to be worthless, and never buy anything else from that manufacturer.

The technical writers who prepare those instructions have become indispensable to industry.

### . . . About Aerospace-Defense Products

In addition to consumer and industrial products, American industry makes most of the products for aerospace and defense—fighter aircraft, space vehicles, radar sets, tactical radio sets, and tanks. Such work is done by industry under contract with the federal government, using funds budgeted by the President of the United States and appropriated by the Congress.

There must be instructions for operation and maintenance for those products, too. But because of their complexity, the instructions may be quite extensive. For example, the instructions for a military radar set are much greater in volume than those for a motorcar (see Fig. 2).

In addition to instructions for the complex equipment it manufactures, a company that obtains government contracts will have to produces several other types of "paperwork" in the process. It will have to prepare proposals to obtain the contracts in the first place. Then it will have to produce progress reports, test plans, test results reports, reliability and quality assurance data, and spare parts lists before the contract is properly completed. Most such paperwork is either written by or edited and produced by technical writers.

### . . . *About Progress*

As a technical program gathers momentum, many kinds of writing need to be done about what is going on right now. Sponsors must be told how the work is going. Management must have the informa-

*Fig. 2. A defense product usually requires more data than a consumer product. A stack of manuals for a radar set is compared to an automobile shop manual.*

tion it needs for planning decisions. Other scientists and engineers need to be told what tests have been made and what the results were so that they won't spend time and money making the same tests to find out the same things. New devices and systems must be documented so that other designers who may want to do similar things will know about that way of doing them.

All those needs, and others, are filled by one or another type of technical report. Many technical writers spend their entire careers working only on various kinds of reports. But those reports differ from one another so much in content, in format, and in method of preparation that even this career maintains its interest and its challenge.

### . . . to Promote Industry

When a research or development program results in a new device or product, the company wants to tell people about it. To do so, they employ a public relations staff whose job it is to prepare press releases and background data for feature stories, provide appropriate photographs or drawings, and arrange press conferences and television interviews. For companies whose business involves science and technology, the job of the public relations staff is essentially that of science writing. For profit-making companies, not only must new products be hailed in the press, but all the company's products must be advertised to promote sales. Again, for scientifically and technically oriented companies, the job of the advertising copywriter can require as much technical knowledge as it does creative ingenuity.

### You May Write for the Government

Technical writers are found throughout the federal government and also, to a lesser extent, in state and local governments.

In the federal government there are perhaps 2,500 "technical writers and editors" in that relatively new government job classification. In addition to that core of technically trained writers and editors, there are in federal service perhaps another 8,000 writers or editors who do script writing for the public media, or who are public information specialists, or visual information specialists, or printing and publications officers, or who in some other way contribute materially to the process of transmitting ideas from one mind to another.

### You May Work on a Newspaper or News Magazine

If you decide you want to be a science writer, the chances are you will work for a newspaper or a news magazine. We think it is fair to say that a science writer is a journalist first, a science writer second. Thus, the science writer will normally serve the usual newspaper or magazine apprenticeship as a general reporter before he is able to try his hand at the reporting of scientific or medical news.

That contrast brings up another worth noting. Among technical writers, most write either about the physical sciences and engineering or about the biological sciences and medicine, but not about both, whereas the average science writer must span the entire spectrum of human knowledge from medicine through biological research and the physical sciences to engineering. He must be able to write effectively about archeological explorations in the pyramids and in the caves bordering the Dead Sea as well as vibrantly about man's latest exploit on the moon. One assignment may deal with the miracles of open-heart surgery; the next with the biological effects of thermal pollution from a nuclear reactor.

Not only must the science writer deal with that vast array of knowledge, but he must so write about it that the average layman will understand at least the basic problem and the basic achievement, yet so that the educated layman will feel informed rather than belittled. To accomplish that goal, the science writer's writing must be of exceptional quality.

*You May Work for a Book Publisher or Trade Magazine*

There are dozens of book publishers and hundreds of trade magazines. Many of them specialize in scientific, technical, or engineering subjects or have science or engineering departments. Each one requires dozens of writers and editors.

If you were to work for a book publisher, you would probably start out, at least, doing meticulous copy-editing of authors' manuscripts. As you became familiar with the business, you might work into editorial sales, consulting with authors, evaluating manuscripts, and recommending new publishing ventures to management.

If you have an opportunity to work for a trade magazine, you will undoubtedly spend untold hours scanning press releases on new products to find a few items appropriate for inclusion in your next issue. But you will also do more exciting things, such as attending conferences to report on new discoveries in your field, interviewing scientists or engineers about their research projects, or interviewing industrial managers about their newest devices or about future prospects for the industry.

In both areas, you can make important contributions to the dissemination of knowledge. Many of the technical books published are used as texts from which other young people will learn about science. Others will be used as reference works for the working scientist and engineer. In both cases their integrity and accuracy are of utmost importance.

The technical material that is put in books is, in general, well-established, thoroughly researched information that is not likely to be subject to significant changes. Thus, it tends to be rather old material. The material that is included in trade magazines, on the other hand, is the new information that the engineer or scientist needs to keep up-to-date with his field. Here he finds the data on new tests, new theories, new materials that he needs to keep pace with his competitors. Thus, books and trade magazines are opposite ends of the same basic educational spectrum. The engineer begins his education with books to find out the past history of his field; he continues his education all his life with trade magazines to find out its present developments.

## You May Work in a Writing Agency

Writing agencies have been among the largest employers of technical writers. There have been more than three hundred such agencies throughout the country offering writing, editing, illustrating, and printing services. As demands for agency services from space and defense contractors crested a few years ago, most agencies have had to cut back their staffs; some have had to close. Many agencies are still active, however, and are doing a brisk business. To some extent, the more recent defense and space cutbacks have helped the agencies, since industrial and research-and-development organizations are tending to hold down their own staffs and use agencies for their overloads.

That technique is typical of the way agencies have always been used. Most companies maintain some writing, editing, illustrating, and printing capacity, but often they need more service than their own organization can supply. They then turn to an agency for help. Some few organizations maintain no internal publications staff and must rely entirely on agencies for their publication output.

Agencies vary greatly in the way they handle the people who work for them. Some maintain large in-house staffs, others almost none. Some maintain large groups of on-call people who come in to work when needed, but otherwise stay home. Others have large groups of staff members working in local industrial and research-and-development plants on a contract basis.

The value of an agency is based on three abilities: it can do the job the customer needs done; it can produce a high-quality product; and it can meet tight (often, well-nigh impossible) deadlines.

Thus, one of the prime selling points of most agencies is their ability to turn out a creditable product in almost any area of technical communication. Most agencies embody that sort of wide-ranging versatility in their top managers or owners who have done all the jobs themselves at one time or another. Those remarkably competent people can and do advise and guide less experienced members of the in-house staff.

Because of the versatility and competence of the top managers, and because of the opportunity to learn from these leaders in the field, an agency can be an excellent training ground for a technical writer, editor, or illustrator.

An example of a successful writing agency is Rosern Publications and Procedures, Inc., in Chicago. In 1955, Rosalie and Ernestine ("ROSERN") Kohn founded a small agency that has since expanded to supply all types of technical and scientific publications. Their success is the result of their individual expertise: Rosalie is a specialist in management and business procedures (essential to the success of any business), and Ernestine is an expert in spare-parts provisioning, technical manuals, and other government contract data.

The two sisters work very hard (see Fig. 3), but they receive the rewards of independence. When business becomes slack, which happens occasionally in any business, they take off and travel the world around.

*You May Work Everywhere—the Free-Lancer*

Technical and science writers who develop special abilities and reputations that are much in demand may become self-employed and sell their services to many separate buyers. They are the *free-lancers,* named after the itinerant knights of old who sold their fighting ability to the highest bidder.

Fig. 3. Personnel of a typical writing agency.

COURTESY ROSERN

The benefits of successful free-lancing are many: higher average income, a greater variety of work, contact with more people, and, most appealing to some people, independence.

But there are drawbacks, too. The free-lancer is, in effect, a one-man business who must by himself perform all the functions of a business—selling, self-management, production, and accounting and fee collection. Also, he must take care of his own social security payments, insurance, and self-employment taxes. One person often finds it difficult to find time for all those activities.

Another drawback has been pointed out by Larry McCombs, who has free-lanced in educational writing:

> Like any free-lance writer, an education science writer suffers from an uneven income. Until you are established, you cannot count on a steady supply of work. Good opportunities are apt to arrive in batches when you cannot accept all of them. Then when you need work, nothing may turn up.

*Other Places You May Work*

Technical and science writers work in many other places. Here are a few more examples:

- *In Educational Institutions.* More and more writers are finding jobs in universities and other centers of learning such as medical and dental schools. Many universities have special scientific research divisions that need writing help, as well as their regular faculty researchers. In addition, the advent of government support for university research has added the requirement for periodic progress reports that scientists rarely can take time for.
- *In Pharmaceutical Research and Manufacturing Laboratories.* Here new developments must be described and promoted, tests must be reported, and the requirements of the Public Health Service for the certification of new drugs must be complied with.
- *In Medical Laboratories.* Here reports must be made on each ebb and flow of the tide of battle against a disease, since one can never predict which results will be truly significant in the

long run. Sometimes, of course, press releases must be written to announce the occasional breakthroughs.

In all those places technical and science writing is being done. As you can see from even this brief survey, the field is one that offers wide variety in subject matter, in type of work done, and even in life style while you are doing it.

So, if you are interested in words, their meanings, and their combinations, and if you are interested in some aspect of science, engineering, biology, or medicine, and if combining the two interests into a career appeals to you, you will surely be able to find some aspect of technical or science writing that is your special "bag."

# CHAPTER III

# How You Will Communicate

Technical and science writers communicate information. The source of the information is the engineer, scientist, biologist, or physician who creates it in the course of his work. The writer is the bridge —the transmitter—who conveys that information to other engineers, researchers, doctors, or managers, or to the general public. As we all do, the writer communicates through symbols. He uses three basic kinds of symbol: words, pictures, and specialized arbitrary signs.

## You Will Communicate with Words

Many kinds of words are of interest to the technical and science writer. The first group that comes to mind—the technical words relating to the special subject matter he happens to be talking about— are important for him to understand, but are not really the most important in his working life. Unless he is writing for another scientist in the same narrow specialty, each of those technical words must be translated into more common technical language so they can be properly understood.

Thus, the second type of word that concerns the technical and science writer is the ordinary technical word that is part of the working vocabulary of most educated laymen—*feet, yards, meters, double helix, ovum, space capsule, light-year,* and so on. Such words the technical writer can use to most of his audiences without explanation, but many of them the science writer must still explain to his.

The third type of word that the technical and science writer needs —and perhaps the most important—is the ordinary word. The ordinary nouns and verbs and adjectives; the prepositions, conjunctions, and articles; those are the words in which every story is really told. They are the words everyone understands.

We are tempted to say that this is everyman's speaking language, but really it is a bit more elegant than that. (If you have ever listened with a critical ear to someone speaking "off the cuff," the chances are that what you heard were disconnected strings of words that did not form sentences and, at best, managed to convey a general feeling about the speaker's subject.) So the everyday language we speak of might be called "laundered shirt-sleeve English," that is, shirt-sleeve English that has been cleaned up enough to have it make sense when you see it in print. It is the language every writer must master, even the technical writer, and especially the science writer.

The importance of using words effectively cannot be overemphasized. Although a major part of everyone's education, beginning with the first words of a toddler and continuing all through school, has been devoted to communicating with words, most people neither use words particularly well nor find writing an easy occupation. The importance of words is reemphasized by the fact that they are not only tools of communication but arc also essential elements of the thought process as well. Most everyday working concepts and most scientific ideas are put together largely as words in the mind. The mind's output is also in words, which, hopefully, will be logically arranged for quick comprehension by the reader or listener. (Of course, we must not overgeneralize. The output of some concepts is music or a painting or a structure.)

But writing is the prime tool of the technical and science writer. He must be able to write well and easily. His prose must be accurate, his words precise, his phraseology unobtrusive. He must be able to make complicated sets of facts clear and understandable without oversimplifying. He must be economical in his use of words and able to eliminate verbosity in the writing of others. He must have an intuitive feel for the lilt and rhythm of the language and must use that intuition to make his language flow smoothly from sentence to sentence. He must enjoy working with the language, be interested in the precise meanings of words, and be dedicated to making language communicate rather than conceal.

Thus, the technical or science writer is a rare breed. He has had sufficient interest and ability in science or engineering or medicine to obtain some in-depth training or education in one of those specialties. But he also has a genuine interest in language: its meanings, its shadings, its nuances, its structure, and its use as a vehicle for communication. He must, further, be willing to set aside any ambitions he might have had of becoming a working scientist, and be willing to accept with equanimity a supporting role, though a very necessary one, in which he works more with words and stories of scientific achievement than with science or engineering itself.

### *You Will Communicate with Pictures*

Sometimes pictures originate with the scientist, engineer, or physician who hands in a series of more or less rough sketches or a series of photographs with his manuscript. Sometimes it is up to the writer to provide suitable illustrations for his story. Often he can do so satisfactorily only in collaboration with an illustrator or in collaboration with an illustrator and a photographer.

Often the scientist or engineer will submit every graph and photograph the project has produced for inclusion in the report. Then the writer or editor's problem is how to reduce the illustrations to a reasonable number without hurting the author's feelings. At the other extreme, a writer may be working on a story in which, to explain properly the functions of a nuclear reactor, he needs a cutaway drawing of the plant or a photograph of it when partially completed. But by the time he gets the assignment, the plant is built, closed in, inaccessible, and all that is left are blueprints. So, he must take the blueprints to an illustrator and work with him to help him produce a cutaway drawing of the plant.

From those examples, it is clear that writers have problems with pictures and must know enough about the various types of pictures that can be made, how they are made, and how they are used, to be able to direct the illustrating activity for any writing project they work on.

Preparing illustrations for publication always requires the help of a good, professional illustrator, and sometimes of a skilled technical photographer as well. In working on a report or a story, the writer and illustrator, at the very least, should work as a team. They should decide together which parts of the story can best be told in words, which in illustrations. The illustrator can often be of untold help in tailoring illustration techniques to meet cost limitations, in advising on how best to use a touch of color, and in selecting the right type of illustration (see Fig. 4) to tell the pictorial part of the story forcefully and quickly.

The writer does not create the actual artwork. On the other hand, he may make rough sketches or explain to the illustrator in words what he wants. He will always edit art sketches submitted by an author. The artwork is made by three specialists: the draftsman, the photographer, and the illustrator.

The draftsman creates two-dimensional representations such as mechanical drawings, electrical schematics, and block diagrams. The photographer takes pictures of any subject the writer may specify, from microscopic cells to an oil refinery filling many acres. His versatility and ingenuity may often be taxed to create photographs that will show the precise point needed to supplement the text.

The illustrator is a combination of draftsman and creative artist. His major work is in making realistic representations of subjects, showing them in perspective, "exploded," or in "cutaway" views to show internal workings. Also, the illustrator knows how to blend text and illustrations into an attractive and readable format that tells its message effectively. He knows how to prepare text and illustrations for reproduction by a variety of techniques. He is a primary working partner of the creative technical writer. Scientist, writer, and illustrator form the inseparable communications team.

## You Will Communicate with Arbitrary Signs

Some arbitrary signs are so familiar as to be commonplace. Everyone knows what "$+$," "$-$," "$\times$," and "$\div$" mean when used with numbers. More advanced mathematics uses other signs such as "$\int$," "$\Sigma$," "$\rightarrow$," "$\|$," and others. Then each scientific discipline has its own set of signs, which, like mathematical signs, are used as shorthand abbreviations for particular operations peculiar to those disciplines (see Fig. 5). Often letters from other alphabets, especially the Greek and Hebrew alphabets, are used to represent certain qualities or functions and so act much the same as arbitrary signs.

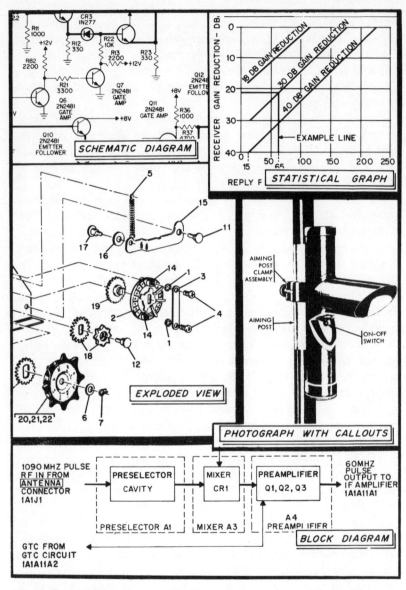

*Fig. 4. Typical illustrations specified by writers and prepared by illustrators.*

COURTESY LARRY HEGG, ILLUSTRATOR,
ZENITH RADIO CORPORATION

In some scientific disciplines, the same is true with certain letters of the English alphabet—when used in certain contexts they become special signs with special meanings.

Every specialty you deal with in science and technology, whether it be in the physical or in the biological sciences, will have its own

*Fig. 5. An assortment of arbitrary signs from a variety of disciplines.*

set of arbitrary signs that has been developed over the years to meet its own needs and, more often than not, is still developing. You must learn those special signs if you are to work or write in the field. In most cases, the list is not too long and at least the well-established parts of it can be found in the back of the dictionary or in other standard reference works.

*You Will Have Guides to Follow*

Whenever you set out to write anything, you will have guides to follow: examples of how it has been done before and descriptions of how it should be done.

Almost always, your own organization will have published a similar document before. If not, other organizations almost certainly will have. By looking back at what has been done before, both at your own company and by others, you can gain insight into how the job should be done, and probably get some good ideas about how what has been done before at your company can be improved.

In addition, your company may have issued its own writing guide or style guide to help its authors, editors, typists, and illustrators work together to put out effective publications. The goal of a style guide is not (as you might at first think) to set standards for the lilt, tempo, and rhythm of language use, but rather to ensure consistency in the details of usage among a given group of editors or within a given series of publications. Thus, the style guide sets up rules for spelling: When do you use "disk," when "disc"; for hyphenation: Do you use "X ray," "X-ray," or "Xray"; for punctuation: Do you say "the flag was red, white, and blue" or "the flag was red, white and blue"; for use of numbers: Do you say "the 8-ohm resistor" or "the eight-ohm resistor"; the component order and punctuation of references and bibliographic entries; and a variety of similar details.

The reason for having such guides is that, although it may make little difference to the reader which way each of these details is handled, it is very annoying to the careful reader if a single book or article jumps randomly back and forth among several possible alternatives from one occurrence to the next. If you have several writers and editors in one company, it is impossible to maintain consistent usage of any convention unless it is written down where all can refer to it.

Beyond such company-related guides, you will also have available many general reference works on the English language. Probably the single most valuable and most frequently used one will be your dictionary. Not only can it help you to pin down proper spellings, but it contains both denotative and connotative word meanings, notes on proper word usage, synonyms, antonyms, and guides to pronunciation. So, for one-stop shopping for information about the English language, the dictionary is hard to beat.

The writer's best guide to the intricacies of such topics as typeface, layout, illustration, design, and photography is his local illustrator.

If you work for the government or for a government contractor, particularly in the defense or space fields, you will find out early whether the government has laid down any specific format guidelines for the document you are assigned to work on, what they are, and how strictly they must be followed. In an effort to minimize costs and increase publication uniformity, both the Defense Department and the National Aeronautics and Space Administration (NASA) have set forth a number of formatting guidelines for various types of publication they require. Some are strict rule books, others are just general guides, and the technical writer must know how much he is bound by them.

# CHAPTER IV

## *Tools You Will Need*

Just as the carpenter must know how to use hammer and saw, so must the technical and science writer know how to use the tools of his trade. His two prime tools are knowledge of the fundamental principles of natural science and skill in the techniques of effective writing.

How are those tools acquired? First, by knowing and understanding what they are and what their value is. Second, by developing a course of study, probably based on a formal academic curriculum, that will give you those tools. Unfortunately, that is much more easily said than done. Very few colleges offer curricula specifically designed to produce technical or science writers. Nevertheless, at almost any college it is possible to develop a curriculum that will give you the tools you need and that will still be acceptable to the school authorities. This chapter will tell you what tools you will need; Chapter VIII will suggest some of the various approaches that can be used in adapting existing curricula to the needs of the would-be technical or science writer.

*Prime Tool: Knowledge of Science and/or Technology*

Scientific knowledge is the foundation for a career in technical or science writing. In the scope and depth of their knowledge, both the technical and the science writer are more *generalists* than are the engineer, scientist, biologist, and physician. Writers have a general understanding of a wide range of scientific knowledge, but lack the detailed knowledge that each active researcher has of his specialty.

There is good reason for such generality. The writer must be able to respond to a wider variety of challenges. He must be able to write on many scientific and technical subjects after only a relatively brief period in which to acquaint himself with the details of a particular specialty. His ability to comprehend quickly is built upon a knowledge of the fundamentals of science and engineering.

We believe that a sound knowledge of basic scientific principles is a vital part of the education of every technical and science writer. The *technical-writer* candidate can safely select physical science *or* biological science *or* engineering. He should take enough so that he gets some laboratory work and learns the basic methods that are used in natural science. (Sometimes, the scientific method can best be learned from the perspective of a course in the philosophy of science.) The would-be *science writer* should take a journalism curriculum with as much science crammed in around the edges as he can manage.

### Prime Tool: Writing Skill

The second of the prime tools is writing skill. Writing can be divided into three categories: utilitarian, utilitarian plus personality, and creative.

*Utilitarian writing* reports, describes, instructs, explains, and teaches. The manual writer uses it when telling how to repair a TV set or an automobile. The pharmaceutical writer uses it in preparing a report on a new drug for a medical journal. The report writer uses it in preparing a progress report for management.

The prime characteristic of utilitarian writing is that it does its job without the injection of the writer's personality. Usually, it is aimed at an audience of readers with special interests, those who know the special language of the field, and have the depth of knowledge essential to comprehend the message.

Technical writing is utilitarian.

Despite the humdrum flavor of the term "utilitarian," the world could not do without this style of writing. In describing that new drug in his utilitarian words, the pharmaceutical writer may be contributing to the saving of countless lives. All things comprehensible to the mind of man can be conveyed by utilitarian writing, from the simplest to the most profound.

Here is an example of utilitarian writing that describes one of the most dramatic moments in all history—man's first landing on the moon. It is from NASA's 22nd Annual Report to Congress.

> The spacecraft circled the moon for a day, then the lunar module (LM), with Astronauts Armstrong and Aldrin aboard, separated from the Command and Service Module (CSM) and descended toward the lunar surface.

> To this point, the Apollo 11 mission was much the same as Apollo 10. In the descent to the lunar surface, however, there were dramatic differences. During the final approach phase, the crew saw that the LM was headed for the general area of a large, rugged crater, filled with boulders five to ten feet in diameter. Commander Armstrong took manual control and guided the LM to a landing approximately 1,000 feet farther downrange.

> As the LM settled on the lunar surface with a slight jolt at 4:18 p.m. on July 20th, Armstrong radioed mission control "The Eagle has landed." (The LM was named Eagle, the CSM Columbia.)

From the above example, it is clear that utilitarian writing communicates its message in a businesslike way, impersonal and precise.

The second form is also utilitarian and businesslike, but is not so impersonal—there is a "plus" added.

*Utilitarian plus personality:* Here the writer's own special approach to telling the story becomes important. The reader is attracted by the way the story is told as well as by its content. In this kind of writing we forsake the utterly matter-of-fact approach and inject suspense and excitement into our writing.

Science writing is utilitarian writing with the added plus. Examples are innumerable in newspaper and magazine journalism, in advertising copywriting, in television and radio—all rely upon the personalities of their writers. The depth of coverage is usually not as great as with straight utilitarian writing, since the readers are the general public rather than scientists or engineers. The audience is much greater, however, because there are so many more of the "general public."

The world could get along without utilitarian-plus writing, but it would be a much duller place.

Here is an example of utilitarian-plus writing. Again it is an account of the same moon landing, this time by aviation/space writer Peter Reich, for the newspaper *Chicago Today*:

> Now they were nearing the climax of that fantastic journey, a scant two miles above the moon's dry Sea of Tranquility. It was July 20, 1969.
>
> A computer flies the Eagle issuing electronic commands that cause stabs of flame to spurt silently from guidance rockets— little bursts of power that position the craft in the airless void of space and guide it towards a touchdown on the lunar surface.
>
> Armstrong and Aldrin, standing at the controls, streetcar-motor-man fashion, monitor the computer's work.
>
> But the computer errs!
>
> Moments from touchdown, it is guiding Eagle into a rock-strewn crater that Armstrong later describes as the size of a football field and strewn with boulders the size of Volkswagens! Less than a minute from disaster, Armstrong disconnects the computer and assumes manual control of his craft.
>
> Coolly, deliberately, he stems Eagle's descent and guides it onward, beyond the rim of the yawning crater, over another rocky expanse, to an open plain.
>
> At 3:17 p.m., Chicago time, words go out by radio that electrify Earthlings 238,000 miles away:
>
> "Houston, Tranquility Base here—the Eagle has landed."

Although the topic is the same, there is a wide difference between the style of NASA and the style of Peter Reich. Reich's version would be resented in a sober report to Congress, whereas NASA's version would command little readership in a newspaper. However, each has its place and each has its value in that place.

To provide the plus that science writing needs, the science writer must have a vivid imagination and a good sense of what aspects of an event will excite the interest of the layman. But combined with imagination, the science writer must also exercise discretion, judgment, and taste so that his story remains basically factual and free from distortions that would inflame public opinion, arouse unfounded public hopes, or express personal opinions disguised as factual reporting. He must also have a fine command of the English language. He must know just the right word to use to evoke the image he wants or to convey the proper nuance of meaning to the reader. To be really good at science writing, the writer's command of the language, particularly toward the literary end of the linguistic spectrum, must be better than that usually required of the technical writer.

*Creative writing* is where the magic happens—where the material of everyday life and living takes on a special quality by passage through the mind of the creative writer. Although it is impossible to define adequately this sort of creativity, and although it can assume as many varied forms as there are creative writers, the end product is readily recognizable as a unique human value.

Science and technology are fit subjects for the creative writer, and there have been impressive examples of creative writing about scientific subjects, such as this excerpt from Rachel Carson's *The Sea Around Us*:

> . . . the sea lies all about us. The commerce of all lands must cross it. The very winds that move over the lands have been cradled on its broad expanse and seek ever to return to it. The continents themselves dissolve and pass to the sea, in grain after grain of eroded land. So the rains that rose from it return again in rivers. In its mysterious past it encompasses all the dim origins of life and receives in the end, after, it may be, many transmutations, the dead husks of that same life. For all at last return to the sea—to Oceanus, the ocean river, like the ever-flowing stream of time, the beginning and the end.[1]

---

[1] Rachel Carson, *The Sea Around Us* (New York: Oxford University Press, 1948).

Those who can write creatively about science and technology will find a great audience of readers and viewers awaiting them.

But back to the bread-and-butter of it.

Because writing is a prime tool of his trade, the would-be technical or science writer must start at once to gain mastery over the English language. He must learn the conventional rules by which it is put together; he must broaden his vocabulary; he must become sensitive to the shades of meaning among nearly synonymous words; he must develop an awareness of the rhythm and flow of language. To learn those things, he must read widely, study assiduously, live with his dictionary, and practice his writing at every opportunity.

He should write and have his writing criticized, and write again, until producing good prose is as routine as tying a shoe. He should write well instinctively, yet with full understanding of why his writing is correct. If he cannot, he is as incompetent as the carpenter who cannot hammer a nail straight. No matter how great his technical competence, he should not try to become a technical or science writer if he cannot handle language easily and effectively.

*Secondary Tools*

These are the tools that, when combined with the primary tools of scientific knowledge and writing ability, complete the picture of the technical or science writer.

*Pictorializing.* Every writer, particularly one who is dealing with technical or scientific material, must know how to use illustrations effectively to complement his text. He must know when the reader really needs an illustration to help him understand the text. He must know which one of the great variety of possible types of illustration will be best in each situation. He must be mindful of the cost both of drawing the illustration and of reproducing it. He must understand reproduction techniques and must select illustration techniques that will reproduce well however his text is being reproduced.

In report and magazine writing, the writer or editor usually has considerable freedom in illustration selection. In newspaper writing, the writer may be handicapped by not having ready access to an illustrator. In the preparation of manuals, the writer may find that his sponsor's specifications dictate what illustrations he shall use.

In some communication media, pictures are used to tell the story as much as, or more than, words. When a writer is preparing a motion picture, film-strip, or television production, his success depends upon his ability to flow visual images together in a meaningful fashion, lacing them together with a thread of words.

Whatever the form of communication, effective use of visual material is an essential part of the process.

*Diplomacy.* The writer does not work in isolation. He is constantly working with other people. A science writer must often obtain his entire story from a working scientist in the course of an interview. A technical writer must ask scientists or engineers questions about their work. He often must suggest extensive rewriting of an engineer's draft or must suggest that a scientist's wording should be revised to avoid ambiguity. He must point out typists' errors without offending them and must persuade them to correct errors he overlooked in an earlier draft. He must discuss proposed illustrations with illustrators and achieve a meeting of minds on how the illustrations should be handled. In all such contacts with other people, he must exercise restraint and persuasion, must be willing to compromise, and must, in general, handle himself with that diplomatic aplomb that results from easy professional self-confidence.

Sometimes a writer will have to conduct a more or less formal interview with a scientist or engineer. Before going to see him, the writer should familiarize himself with the subject-matter area they are going to be talking about. Such preparation permits the writer to understand the scientist more readily, improves the writer's professional image in the scientist's eyes, and avoids wasting interview time on general background data. The first few minutes of the interview are usually devoted to the pleasantries of getting acquainted and establishing a friendly atmosphere for the interview. Then the writer begins questioning the scientist about his work, guides him from one stage to the next without letting him dwell too long on intricate and unreportable details. But throughout the interview, the writer's primary function and chief asset is to *listen*—that is the highest compliment one professional can pay another.

*Typing and Shorthand.* For a reporter, which both technical and science writers are, certain minimal, but not universal, mechanical skills are essential. He must be able to get words on paper relatively quickly in a form that someone else can use easily.

The two primary ways of doing that are neat handwriting and touch typing. Handwriting is relatively slow (speeds range from 27 to 34 words per minute). As your speed increases, your legibility decreases. Nevertheless, some people find that their thoughts flow more easily when they are writing than when they are typing or dictating. They probably feel that way simply because we all learned first to write by hand and so are most familiar with that set of reflexes.

For the professional writer, however, learning to use a typewriter by the touch method is absolutely essential. Even beginners can type faster than 35 words per minute, and experienced typists reach speeds of more than 100 words per minute. Beside the added speed, typing guarantees legibility, which is a great asset when you are immediately handing your material on to another person for further processing.

Nevertheless, handwriting cannot be discarded entirely. Most editing is done by hand on a typed manuscript and then is retyped by someone other than the editor. For that reason, the writer-editor's handwriting must remain legible. In some cases, it even becomes important to revert to hand printing rather than using script when clarity is particularly important.

There are occasions when fast, accurate transfer of someone else's words is important to a writer. Usually it occurs in an interview situation when time is precious and the subject's fleeting words must somehow be captured. For that, normal handwriting is too slow, the typewriter too bulky and noisy. Often you are then reduced to jotting down a few key words or phrases as notes and relying largely on memory until you can get away to record your recollections more fully and permanently.

If you foresee (or discover on the job) that you are going to have to do a lot of interviewing in which capturing extended, accurate quotations is essential, you may find it worthwhile to study a formal shorthand such as the Gregg or A-B-C type. For ordinary language, those shorthands can increase your recording speed up to about 120 words per minute, with normal speeds running 80 to 100. If the material you are trying to record contains a lot of technical words with which you are unfamiliar, your speed will drop sharply. Your speed and accuracy will also fall off quickly if you do not use your shorthand frequently. Thus, for the writer, as opposed to the stenographer, the considerable investment in time, effort, and expense that a shorthand course represents may not be worthwhile.

Another way around the problem is the development of your own personal set of abbreviations to speed up your note-taking process. But perhaps a better solution has been handed us by modern technology. The modern transistorized tape recorder can be an ideal interview instrument. It is self-contained, unobtrusive, quiet, accepts information as fast as your subject cares to talk, and makes no mistakes. It is, indeed, the perfect listener. Blank cassettes are available in lengths up to ninety minutes and longer—ample for the ordinary interview.

## Self-Management

The task of writing is a solitary business. When the writer has gathered all available input information, he withdraws into himself and calls up all his resources. There, inside himself, he becomes his own manager, making countless decisions as to how information should be presented and what words it should be couched in. He is his own taskmaster who insists upon reviewing and rewriting, who checks for quality, who pumps up the adrenalin to get the task finished by the deadline.

That is effective self-management. Considering the complexity of the human personality, and the intricacy of the thought process that produces writing, attaining the ability to manage yourself effectively is a real achievement.

Self-management can be learned—it *must* be learned, if you are to become a writer.

## . . . and Last of All

To the capabilities described in this chapter, add these requisites: initiative, dedication to the job at hand, persistence in the face of frequent frustration—and the technical or science writer's bag of tools is now complete.

# CHAPTER V

# You May Be a Technical Writer

Technical writing is writing about engineering, science, medicine, or some other technical subject for an audience that is trained—at least to some degree—in that particular field. The technical writer may be writing about nuclear reactors for nuclear physicists, about a missile guidance radar for a crew of maintenance technicians, about coal-mine-safety procedures for coal miners, about corn borers for farmers, or about a bone-setting procedure for orthopedic surgeons. In all those cases, diverse as they appear, the technical writer is transmitting technical information to a trained technical specialist who may take specific actions as a result of obtaining the information.

Because he is writing for people trained in the specialty he is writing about, he can use a narrower, more specialized vocabulary than he could in writing for the general public. Among the examples we have cited, the writing will vary considerably in its degree of sophistication and in the complexity and extent of its technical vocabulary. The material prepared for the physicists and the surgeons, for example, is likely to be much less comprehensible to the layman than that prepared for the miner or the farmer. But even the latter material will use expressions with which the layman is not familiar if he lacks training in that particular specialty.

## How Many People Do This?

In 1968 it was estimated that there were close to 25,000 technical writers in the country.[1] At that time it was the judgment of the pub-

---

[1] V. M. Root, "Technical Publications Job Patterns and Knowledge Requirements," *Technical Communications*, Third Quarter, 1968, pp. 5–12.

lications supervisors contacted that moderate growth in the field would characterize the two succeeding years. During that two-year period, government spending for defense and space projects has dropped significantly, continuing a trend that was already evident in 1968. If we interpret "moderate growth" as approximately 5 percent for the two-year period, the addition of that percentage would probably not fall outside the probable error range of the original estimate, so we still may say that there are probably approximately 25,000 technical writers and editors in the country today.

*The Years Ahead.* As we write, the nation finds itself in a period of readjustment, a period for taking stock of its activities and for reestablishing its perspectives and its priorities. Unemployment of scientists and engineers is a symptom of that readjustment. As we sort things out and decide how we need to use science and engineering in the service of our new national goals, not only will the unemployment of those men and women be a thing of the past, but we can safely predict that the need for new scientists and engineers will resume a pattern of growth. The use of such specialties will not be so highly concentrated in defense and space activities as it has been in the recent past, but the greater diversity will make for a healthier scientific community.

As the demand for scientific and engineering personnel begins to grow again, so will the demand for technical writers, editors, and illustrators. Even with very modest growth rates of 2 to 3 percent per year the number of technical writers will double by the year 2000. If any type of scientific effort should catch the public imagination and be heavily funded by the Congress, the next three decades could see the nation's technical writers numbering close to 75,000.

It is obvious, therefore, that the career of technical writing is one well worth considering if you have the right combination of interests and talents. The need for your services will be increasing as the years go by, since, as we have said, people with the right combination of talents are relatively rare—rarer certainly than the scientists and engineers with whom they work.

### What Do Technical Writers Do?

The technical writer's goal is to take information from an authoritative technical source and convey it clearly, unambiguously, accurately. It must be written at a level appropriate to the intended receiver. A technically trained user must be able to accept the information as a reliable, undistorted guide for action.

To do so, the writer may:

- have to interview a scientist.
- work with a group of engineers as they build equipment.
- be handed a scientist's or engineer's manuscript.

Regardless of how he gets his information, his next step is always the same. He reviews the information to determine how best to organize it. In making his decision, he takes into account the nature of the information, the primary audience for whom it is intended, the physical medium through which it will be conveyed, and any external constraints under which he is working. If the job is large and complicated, the organization process can take a substantial amount of time and effort. If he is handed a manuscript that a scientist has already organized quite well, the organization process may be reduced to a nod of approval.

Once the organization is decided upon, the working with words begins. If you, as the writer, must write a manual from scratch, this word-working involves primarily writing page after page of manuscript. If your job is preparing a condensation for a brief article from a long report, it may involve simply transcribing certain portions of the original report and writing an introduction, a conclusion, and a few transition passages. If you are working with a scientist's manuscript, your job will be basically one of editing—checking technical completeness, the logic of the presentation, and the quality of the writing.

After your initial draft is done, you will go through many rewrites, polishing and rephrasing. But even after you are satisfied with the wording, the job is not done. Now you must go through the manuscript two or three more times to make some mechanical checks. You must be sure that it adheres to your company's and your sponsor's style and format guidelines. You must adjust headings for consistency. You must make sure that the illustrations and tables are in the right order. If you have originated the manuscript, have another technical writer or editor look at it. Your errors will be likely to "jump out of the page" as a new pair of eyes and a fresh mind look at the manuscript.

Next, the manuscript must be prepared for final reproduction. Usually you will have your manuscript typed by a professional manuscript typist for publication. You will be responsible for giving her the instructions and guidance she needs to ensure that the job is done the way you want it. You will also be responsible for seeing that the final version is completely and accurately proofread.

Early in the process of preparing your material you will have given thought to what illustrations you will want to use. By now, you should be getting the completed illustrations back, and you must proofread each one of them just as carefully as the text. If your typists and illustrators are good, their products will be 80 to 90 percent correct the first time, but there will always be a few errors that must be corrected.

At this point, you will probably have to oversee the process of page makeup. You may even have to do it yourself. Usually, however, page makeup is done by an illustrator. As writer or editor, your job in the paste-up stage is to see that the pages and columns of text make sense as they follow one another, that the illustrations are in the proper place and have the correct captions, and that the pages are all properly numbered.

Now, finally, you take one last, long look through the reproduction copy to make sure every page of text, every table, and every illustration is there and in its proper place. When it is, you are ready to send it to the printer.

A few days later, with luck, a sample copy of your report or manual will be on your desk for checking. Once again you go over it with a fine-tooth comb checking for errors: pictures printed upside down, unintentional blank pages, pages out of order, and so on. Then you send the sample copy back for page corrections, assembly, and binding.

When the finished volume arrives, and you look it over and find that it is basically correct, you just can't help sitting quietly for a minute, just staring at it, gently riffling the pages, and letting that warm glow of satisfaction and accomplishment suffuse your being. It has been a lot of work, but it's done; it's good; it's *yours!* The satisfaction is there; it is unmistakable; you've earned your pay;

you've had your reward. That glow inside will probably just about last through the frustrations of your current publication. But that's the joy of it—if it wasn't a struggle to do, the doing of it wouldn't feel so good!

But the warm satisfaction of a job well done may not be the only psychological reward of technical writing. The collection of your original material or the procurement of your illustrations may turn into an exciting adventure. It has, on more than one occasion, for Terry Smith of the Westinghouse Electric Corporation. Here is what he says about some of his varied assignments:

> How would you like to shoot a movie from the open door of a helicopter, or act as a courier to London and Paris, or travel to 24 states and 3 foreign countries? These are just a few of the things I have done as a technical writer, and you could do the same.

> True, most of the time you will find yourself closer to home, but even when you're behind your desk, you'll find excitement in working on important assignments which might include instruction manuals, technical reports, proposals, advertising brochures, and technical films.

In his action-packed career, Terry also found time to write a book (*How to Write Better and Faster,* published by Crowell in 1965) and to lecture widely on report writing and editing. So, you see, there are at least occasional flashes of glamour even in a career based on utilitarian writing.

The jobs technical writers do can be divided into three broad categories: writing in direct support of engineering, writing in general support of engineering and science, and writing and editing for general publication. Within each of those broad categories are several specific types of jobs that we will describe in the following sections.

### Technical Writing in Direct Support of Engineering

#### Instruction Manuals

Preparing such manuals is a prime activity of technical writers, and perhaps more writers are engaged in this than in any other technical writing activity. The federal government alone spends about $1,000,000,000 annually for manuals that describe aerospace-defense equipment, ranging from auto engines to moon vehicles. Manuals for commercial and industrial products are also created in great numbers. They cover just about everything that is operated or can be repaired—trucks, washing machines, television and radio sets, computers, electrocardiographs, aircraft, radars, sonars, meters, and various types of test equipment.

The instruction manual tells and shows how to install, operate, and maintain equipment. It is a very detailed document (see Fig. 6). It describes, and usually shows in photographs or drawings, the physical appearance of the equipment it is dealing with. It explains the overall purpose of using the equipment. It explains the theory upon which the equipment is based. If the equipment is complex

## RULES FOR DISMOUNTING THE RIFLE MUSKET.

### MODEL OF 1863.

1st. Unfix the bayonet (15.)

2d. Put the tompion (45) into the muzzle of the barrel.

3d. Draw the ramrod (5.)

4th. Turn out the tange-screw (3.)

5th. Take off the lock (16;) to do this, first put the hammer at half-cock, then unscrew partially the side-screws (19 a, b,) and, with a slight tap on the head of each screw with a wooden instrument, loosen the lock from its bed in the stock, then turn out the side-screws and remove the lock with the left hand.

6th. Remove the side-screws (19 a, b,) taking care not to disturb the washers (41.)

7th. Take off the upper band (38) by first loosening the screw (e.)

8th. Take off the middle band (39) in the same manner.

9th. Take off the lower band (40) in the same manner.

NOTE.—The letter U on the bands is to indicate the upper side in assembling.

10th. Take out the barrel, (1.)   In doing this, turn the musket horizon-

*Fig. 6. The method for describing disassembly shown in this excerpt from a Civil War manual (1863) is still used for today's complex equipment.*

mechanically, and if someone may need to assemble, disassemble, or repair parts of that mechanism, extremely detailed drawings are presented—usually cutaways or exploded views—that show exactly where each component fits with respect to every other. In addition, step-by-step instructions are provided for assembling or installing the equipment and for checking it out to make sure it is operating properly.

If the piece of equipment is relatively simple, such as, for example, a phonograph turntable assembly, the same manual may include operating instructions and troubleshooting instructions. If the equipment is as complicated as a computer, however, the operation manual will be a separate volume. It must tell the operator how to handle a wide variety of input possibilities and an equally wide variety of possible malfunctions. The maintenance manual is likely to be another separate volume even larger than the operation manual. It will contain a whole series of troubleshooting procedures, each for use with a different set of symptoms to trace down the difficulty most efficiently. It may also contain systems tests to check whether the system is operating properly. If the equipment contains electronic circuitry, the maintenance manual will include complete circuit diagrams.

Instruction manuals of all types must be precisely and meticulously written. In giving assembly instructions, for example, the different parts must be identified and easily distinguishable from one another. In giving troubleshooting or repair instructions care must be taken to distinguish between tests made with the power on and disassembly operations that must be done with power off. Safety precautions must be noted. And the technical terminology used must be tailored to the known level of the people who will be using the manuals. Thus, a skilled former repairman often makes a very good member of a manual-writing team.

The manual writer must be an expert in at least two disciplines. He must have a good working knowledge of engineering practice and some comprehension of engineering theory. He must also be able to describe such theory and practice in terms of words, pictures, and signs, and he must be able to do so with accuracy, precision, and complete lack of ambiguity.

Here are some examples of writing found in instruction manuals:

Description of equipment

Receiver, Radio, Model 726 (hereafter known as the "receiver"), is a lightweight unit that is transistorized to provide low current drain. The receiver can receive signals that are polarized horizontally and vertically, and that are either modulated or unmodulated.

Description of operating theory

The action of the clipper stage and of the preceding AVC circuit assures high average side-band power and constant modulation levels over a wide range of voice signal strengths, and increases the intelligibility of speech when receiving signals of low signal-to-noise ratios.

Description of disassembly

(1) Remove the blower motor assembly from the amplifier as described in subpara. a.

(2) Remove the aluminum backplate (secured by five screws) from the molded blower housing.

(3) Remove the wheel from the motor shaft by . . . (etc.)

In the equipment description you will note the use of a fairly large proportion of technical terms: "transistorized," "low current drain," "polarized," "modulated," and "unmodulated." Probably most of the terms will already be part of the normal working vocabulary of the technically trained audience for whom the manual is being prepared.

The sample disassembly instructions begin to indicate how very detailed and step-by-step such manuals must be. Time and space are saved by not repeating instructions already given elsewhere—note the reference to other instructions in (1). The backplate is identified both by material (aluminum) and by the fact that it is put on with five screws—the front plate may be steel or plastic and attached with three (or eight) screws. Attention to details is a must for the manual writer.

Thus, to be a manual writer you may not need a broad, general education; you may not need a college degree; but you *do* need some formal training in at least one major technical discipline, such as electronics, aircraft engines, automobile engines, or electrical equipment. You will be helped toward a technical-manual-writing career if you have had some technician-level experience in your specialty. You will definitely need some natural and cultivated ability to handle words easily, but you will not have to produce as polished prose as do technical writers who are writing for management or for other engineers. Also, you should have a personality that enjoys paying meticulous attention to a great many details.

As we look into the future, we can see that many changes are on the horizon in the technical manual business. Already, some manuals are never published on paper. Rather, the original pages and illustrations are photographed on cartridge microfilm, and the film cassettes are all that is distributed. In some particularly sophisticated applications, a multiple-cassette-viewer is combined with a computer to help the technician locate what he needs quickly.

Such techniques require some rethinking of the organization and accessibility of manuals, but they are basically changes in storage and retrieval techniques and have only minor influence on the manual's preparation. It still must be written, the illustrations drawn, the proofreading done, and the "reproducibles" prepared. The computers must still be programed and stocked with data. The future may change the transmission media with which the manual writer works, but it will not eliminate his job.

*Parts Documentation*

The documents this writer produces are parts lists, bills of material, catalog lists, and special lists for the purchase of spare parts. He may also create many variations of lists from the basic parts data, such as inventory lists, "buy" lists, preferred vendor lists, preferred parts lists—all of which are valuable to an engineering operation.

When a company works under certain contracts with the federal government, large quantities of spare parts may be required. Those spares are listed on a Provisioning List prepared by a provisioning specialist.

Most parts documentation today is done with the aid of data processing equipment, since any task as repetitive in its entries, as detailed in its nature, and as subject to frequent revision as a parts listing lends itself admirably to electronic data processing. The benefits are faster, more efficient, more error-free, and less expensive handling of parts information.

This career is ideal for one who enjoys working with details, and who is painstakingly accurate. It is often a good starting job to take with a view to gradually breaking into more general technical writing. As the parts lister increases his skill, he becomes a valuable and well-paid member of the engineering publications staff, and he may have opportunities to expand into other technical writing areas.

*Specifications*

In the course of a system development and manufacturing program, it is necessary to prepare documents that are called specifications. Their basic purpose is to ensure component quality and compatibility. Here is an example of how they work.

A corporation has a contract to develop a complicated new system. It turns to a variety of small specialty firms to develop and manufacture many of the pieces that make up the whole system. But the corporation must be sure that each component does the job required of it, lasts long enough, accepts the proper inputs, and produces the proper outputs. (Neglect of these input-output compatibilities could result in a system that, when finally put together, refuses to work at all.)

Thus, the corporation engineers lay out the system and then write up a document for each subcontractor that spells out what inputs his part of the system will receive, what outputs it must provide, and how reliable it must be. A few years ago, the engineers wrote specifications themselves, but recently the job has been taken over almost entirely by specification writers. This type of technical writer works very closely with the design engineers and often must call meetings of engineers to get a decision on certain design tolerances so that he can make his publication deadline. Sometimes, in such a conference, the specification writer, who may himself have an engineering degree, makes personal contributions to the technical decision.

Unfortunately specifications do not stay written. Usually the systems require extensive development. At the start of a development program, even an experienced engineer can do little more than make an educated guess about how well it will be possible to get any of the proposed components to work. As development proceeds, some components fall short of the mark; compensations have to be made;

and the effect of each shortcoming and each compensatory change are felt throughout the system. Specifications have to be revised, rewritten, and revised again. So the specification writer rarely lacks for work.

Many people who succeed as specification writers have engineering degrees, although that is not an absolute requirement. Perhaps more important is their intellectual approach to problems: They tend to take what might be called a legalistic approach. They want to pin down all the possibilities; they want to avoid leaving any loopholes for inferior performance to creep through; they want to spell out not only everything the equipment must do, but also all the conceivable things it might do that it should not. An important asset for the specification writer is the ability to command the respect of engineers; this ability is particularly important when he must call, preside over, and moderate meetings. So long as current contracting procedures persist and so long as complex systems continue to be developed, the need for specification writers will remain.

### Data Managing

In major development and production programs that require parts documentation, technical manuals, and specifications, responsibility for all such types of equipment-supporting data documents may be placed in one department under the direction of a data manager. That unification of responsibility has the advantage that it permits maximum coordination of effort to meet the fluctuating demands of the various parts of the program.

In such an organization, the role of the data manager is, as the name implies, basically one of management rather than of writing. Almost always, however, the data manager is one of the better writers who has had experience in both manual and specification writing and who has proved himself to be a good manager in more modest supervisory positions. That is the route Thomas F. Walton followed as he rose to the position of manager of the Minuteman Program's Technical Data Department at Thompson-Ramo-Wooldridge (TRW) Inc.

The job of a data manager consists of reviewing progress, holding conferences and discussions with members of his staff, writing directives and memoranda of justification for equipment and personnel, making policy decisions, attending management meetings, and evaluating new techniques, approaches, and equipment for data preparation and processing to see if his department's procedures can be improved. Since those are the same activities engaged in by any line manager, Tom Walton, a data-management pioneer, is right when he says, "Manage it as you would hardware."

If you compare the above description of the day-by-day work of the data manager with the descriptions we gave earlier of the specification or manual writer, you will see that it has little in common with either. Yet, as we have said, he must know the jobs of both. The very real differences between the job functions of the data manager and the specification or manual writer point up a problem that occurs in almost every publications organization: publications managers are promoted from the ranks of writers and editors who, generally, have had little training or experience in management. The usual result is that those writers and editors learn management techniques on the job (and become good managers) or ignore the fact that management requires any special knowledge or skill (and become bad managers).

## Technical Writing in General Support of Engineering

### Reports

Reports are used for three purposes: to report progress, to prepare for or report the results of specific tests or experiments (see Fig. 7), and to provide permanent documentation.

Progress reports are usually somewhat fragmentary and so are readily understandable only to those people who are already familiar with what has happened in that program before. Their value is of short duration, since after the next one comes out, few care what happened earlier. To be of value at all, therefore, they must be published and distributed quickly.

Tests or experiments are often performed at remote sites by several organizations working together. So that each contributor will know exactly what part he must play, someone must prepare a test plan some months before the test occurs. Then, afterward, the results

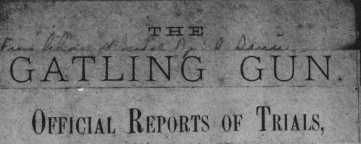

# THE
# GATLING GUN.

## OFFICIAL REPORTS OF TRIALS,

MUSKET CALIBER, TEN BARREL GATLING GUN.
With Carriage and Limber complete.

1,000 yards, and were worked by soldiers who were wholly unused to handling them.

Col. Fletcher says: " From a comparison of a series of eleven trials of the small-sized Gatling, of the 9-pounder muzzle-loading field-gun, firing shrapnel, and of the Martini-Henry rifle, fired by six guardsmen, at ranges from 300 to 1,200 yards, and under various conditions in regard to time and known and unknown distances, I find that the Gatling made 2,699 hits, the 9-pounder

TRIAL OF GATLING 10 BARREL GUN OF 1 IN. CAL.

at Fortress Monroe, October, 1873.

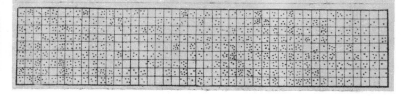

*Fig. 7. Reports have always been essential to the engineering design process. This one, shown in excerpts (cover at top) dates back to 1873. (E. G. Long Collection.)*

must be circulated to all the participants. In the case of experiments done within a single organization, test plans are usually not necessary, and only reports of results are produced.

When a new device has finally been completed, or when a new system has been designed, or when a particular program has been finished, a final summary report must be prepared. Test results and final reports, since they report information that may be good for years instead of only months, are usually prepared with considerably less haste and more care than progress reports. A real effort is made to be sure they are absolutely accurate, that they are easily understandable, and that they contain no possible sources of misinterpretation.

What special talents and training does the report writer need? Because of his relatively close and frequent contact with professional scientists and engineers, a bachelor's degree is almost a must, a master's degree is helpful, and some people with doctorates are in the field. The opportunities for working closely with scientists and engineers will be more readily available to writers with degrees in engineering or science. Opportunities for technical editorial positions have been about equally available to science graduates and to degree holders in English or journalism, but in the future, science and engineering graduates who want to enter the field will probably have the edge. But ability to produce relatively well-polished written material will continue to be a requirement. As for personal characteristics, diplomacy tops the list.

## Proposals

Most government engineering and development programs originate in documents called proposals. A proposal is an offer to perform a certain task—research in molecular fields, development of a new transportation system, design of a lunar vehicle, or manufacture of an aircraft. Usually a proposal describes in detail the benefits to be gained from the proposed development, the theory behind doing the job a certain way, the technical approach to be used, the equipment and facilities required to do the job, the length of time the project is expected to take, and the anticipated costs.

If the proposal is acceptable to the agency that receives it, the agency responds with an OK—a contract or grant that provides funds for doing the job. In the past two decades, the largest producers of proposals have been aerospace and defense firms seeking government contracts. The funds obtained by the proposal technique have exceeded $30,000,000,000 a year. To that sum can be added most of the $17,000,000,000 expended annually by industry for research. Those funds are obtained by engineers and scientists employed by industry, who submit internal proposals to their own managements.

As a result of the need for proposals, a new type of technical writer has appeared—the Proposal Specialist. In addition to the basic requisites of the technical writer—technical knowledge and skill in writing, he must have a special drive that enables him to work under perpetual pressure and to take on the tenth proposal with unquenched enthusiasm, even though the previous nine have been turned down. He must have a generalist's knowledge of the principles of marketing, contract law, accounting, sales and advertising, and of the many forms that proposals may take in applying for contracts and grants. He must know his own company thoroughly, and know the marketplace in which his company sells its wares. He must be able to work well with personnel at all levels to gain their cooperation in the production of an often complex document, since usually a proposal encounters its tight deadline because of the reluctance of a working scientist, budget officer, or top management official to affix the final stamp of approval without just one more revision.

Yet upon his effectiveness depend the jobs of his co-workers and, in a great many cases, the success of the firm that employs him.

The proposal specialist may also prepare presentations—verbal proposals made by an engineer or scientist who lectures on the merits of a proposal for the benefit of potential sponsors. The proposal specialist organizes the presentation and plans and arranges for the preparation of many types of visual aids such as flip charts, viewgraph transparencies, photographic slides, models, and other displays.

## Computer Software Writing

One of the most remarkable and obtrusive developments of the past quarter century, and one without which many others could not have occurred, is the large digital computer.

In the past quarter century, tremendous technological strides have been taken to improve the computers themselves. Their components have been miniaturized to fractions of their original size. Their speed and flexibility have vastly increased. Along with this improvement in the physical computer (which, along with virtually all other physical equipment, shares the shorthand name "hardware") has gone a comparable improvement in the computers' internal programming to provide them with standard internal procedures to simplify job programming and computer operation. By analogy with the term "hardware," the internal programs, which are not hardware such as transistors or resistors, but rather are transient imprints on a small portion of the computer's memory, have been labeled "software."

As John Y. Harrington, a computer software writer for the IBM General Systems Division, in Rochester, N.Y., points out, however, it is not enough to have the professional programmers provide the computer with a variety of automatic internal procedures to do certain jobs for the computer's users. In addition, someone must explain to the user how he is to use the software that has been programed into the computer.

Here is how John describes the work of these highly specialized technical writers:

> Documents developed by software writers tell the reader how to do something with a computer: how to use a particular program, how to write in a particular programming language, how to operate a computer system with a program or a group of programs, or how to locate problems when a program isn't operating correctly. One manual may be developed to teach the basics of data processing to a beginner. Another may be developed by describing in great detail the internal workings of a complex language translator or system supervisor. The skills required to meet this wide range of subject and audience are the same skills required of any professional writer: the ability to write, and a knowledge of the subject you're going to write about.

And here is what John says about the requirements of the career:

> Software writers must have superior ability in the use of the English language. Most employers prefer college graduates with

a major or minor in English or journalism. Also required is the ability to quickly assimilate technical material. *Formal training in data processing is usually not a job prerequisite.* [Italics are the authors'.] Most colleges and universities are now offering courses in computers and data processing, but most companies feel that the detailed programming knowledge required for a specific writing assignment must be acquired on the job. IBM, for example, offers the writer continuing training in programming throughout his career.

John goes on to predict that the need for software writers will increase because, first, many companies have now made software a separate, marketable product, and second, ". . . communication in the technical fields is shaking off the dust and becoming exciting as new graphic communication techniques are being developed."

Indeed, it can be said that almost any career that has to do with computers has great potential. As the prime communicators, writers will always be needed in the field. As with programmers, however, computer software writers must have a love for precision and an infinite capacity for attention to detail, as in the computing business a few small errors can cause interminable delays in getting a program running properly.

## Technical Advertising

As we all know, competition is fundamental to American business practice. Most of the organizations that are involved in the development, engineering, and production of space and defense products are profit-making corporations that make other products for sale in the commercial marketplace. Those commercial products must be developed, engineered, and produced, too, but at company expense. As the final, and absolutely necessary, stage in the process, the products must be sold.

But, unlike the situation even twenty-five years ago, today's products are much more technologically complex. In addition, many of today's buyers are much more aware of, and alert to, subtle technological differences among the products they are offered. Thus, today much advertising copy is so technically sophisticated that the people who prepare it deserve to be called technical writers.

Many companies maintain their own staffs of technical advertising copywriters, but others rely on advertising agencies or on free-lancers. Copywriters prepare advertisements for magazines, brochures describing a product's major virtues, technical data sheets telling in detail what functions the product will perform and what characteristics it has, and direct-mail flyers that often combine many brochure and data-sheet features. Planning advertising can be fun from the graphics viewpoint because advertising budgets usually permit the use of full, glorious color.

Tony Baragona is a technical advertising copywriter, and one of the best. He writes the copy for Motorola's *Collage,* a series of ads that has commanded tremendous readership (see Fig. 8). In response to a request to explain "what you do and how you do it," Tony sent in a five-page stream-of-consciousness thing, which (although it can't be presented in its entirety) is not going to be touched by the authors, lest the flavor of Tony's writing be lost. Here's Tony:

> The problem is to create advertising that is seen, read, and acted upon. That means good, creative, energetic, and innovative people should be doing it.
>
> Technical advertising should be as bright, sprightly, and innovative as it is informative. Some of the best advertising for technical products comes from those who have studied their audience enough to realize that engineers, purchasing agents, scientists, and technical directors have the same sort of glands as everyone else, and that they can be influenced with the same techniques that work in other fields . . . an ad aimed at persuading a technical person to buy a technical product should not look or sound like a catalog sheet. The advertising that "works" most often is that which stands out in some way from the competing ads.
>
> I am also convinced that the writer of technical advertising need not be highly knowledgeable in the technical area he is writing about. If he has access to the engineering and marketing people,

*Fig. 8. Tony Baragona wrote the copy for this advertisement. The product features are listed, but in a form more palatable and interesting than the "specification sheet" approach.* COURTESY MOTOROLA. ADVERTISING MANAGER: EDWARD MC CLELLAN. AGENCY: BOTSFORD-KETCHUM

he can learn what should be said about his product. Too much knowledge is often bad—it results in people making ads that look like spec sheets, that nobody reads.

It's an exciting career, that of an advertising copywriter. And when the subject is technical, there is (as Tony Baragona says) a great challenge in creating that special interest in the subject that will make sales.

So, for the person who aspires to become a technical advertising copywriter, some careful self-evaluation is in order. Is he creative, does he have lots of ideas about how to look at things or present things that seem to be different from the ways other people look at or present them? Ingenuity, distinctiveness—these are the hallmarks of the successful ad man. For the person with bubbling, spontaneous creativity who sees advertising as a challenge yet who has an interest in science or technology, the career of a technical advertising copywriter can provide a lifetime of satisfaction.

## Industrial Audio-Visuals

"Audio-visual" is a relatively new term that covers a wide variety of ways of combining sounds and images. The major such techniques are motion pictures, film-strips (a series of still pictures with accompanying narration), and television. In the future, they will be joined by laser holography—a technique for projecting a three-dimensional image in such a way that the viewer's perspective can be changed at will without the viewer himself moving—and perhaps by similar devices that will give the illusion of placing the viewer within the scene itself.

The currently available techniques are being used in industry for many purposes. Films and TV tapes are being prepared to document certain test or development programs and for training purposes. Audio-visuals are also being used to promote technical sales, to accompany other forms of advertising, and for public relations and public information purposes.

The special capabilities of audio-visual techniques are also being put to good use in education. Children are able to see in motion pictures places, events, and processes that cannot otherwise be re-created in the classroom. Through time-lapse photography they can see the full beauty of an unfolding flower. Through use of language tapes they can hear and imitate authentic foreign accents. Adults, too, need continuing education services, and the medical profession, in which this need is particularly acute, has adapted audio-visual techniques to meet this need. For example, newly developed surgical procedures have been recorded on video tape and then televised along with a subsequent commentary by the surgeon to groups of surgeons at several hospitals all across the country.

The teams that have been assembled for producing audio-visual products vary from organization to organization, but whoever does the job of overall presentation design in a film or tape medium must know not only what pictures to combine with what words, but must also master the transitional visual effects that are available in those media (such as zooms, fades, dissolves, and wipes) and know the emotional and psychic impact of each when used in combination with specific types of subject matter. It is proper use of such visual transitions that does much to establish the mood and vary the pace of the final presentation.

As the sample page of an industrial movie script in Fig. 9 indicates, the script writer and the production designer must either be the same person or must work closely together, for the script itself combines words of narration or dialogue with camera directions, picture descriptions, and soundtrack cues.

Ed Schager, a longtime writer and producer of audio-visuals for industry, says:

Writing is an excellent stepping-stone into this field. Most producers have started as writers because that's where you really learn the business. Then, as you become more proficient as a writer, you are asked to take on more responsibility. There is no better way to master this career.

But Ed sees even more challenges for the audio-visual specialists of the future:

For years we've been using the same old mechanical Kinetoscope invented by Edison in the last century. But now it's going to be a whole new ball game because of the marriage of electronics with pictures.

| PICTURE | SOUND |
|---|---|

CUT TO:

24. MLS. Tree falls. ZOOM TO CU of saw. Finger turns off switch.

SFX. Falling tree, then sound of saw as it is turned off and comes to a stop.

NARRATOR

There . . . the job is done . . . the tree is down in three minutes.

ZOOM BACK:

25. LS. PAN length of tree.

And see—it fell just where the cutter planned. A job done with speed and safety . . .

ZOOM TO:

26. CU. Lumberjack brings saw up to holding position. ZOOM TO ECU of saw.

. . . a job done with the best saw you can buy—the XYZ MARVEL.

*Fig. 9. Typical format of an audio-visual script.*

That's where the future lies now for writers—in their mastery of this new medium of communication.

*Technical Writing for General Publication*

*Technical Magazines*

Magazines that cover a branch of technology are a prime source of practical, right-up-to-the-minute information for engineers and engineering management. Several hundred are published, each covering some portion of contemporary technology. Their scope can be suggested by listing some typical titles:

Aviation Week & Space Technology
Chemical and Engineering News

Data Processing
EDN (formerly Electrical Design News)
Explosives and Pyrotechnics
IEEE Spectrum (A publication of the Institute of Electrical and
Electronics Engineers)
Iron Age
Machine Design
Medical World News
Microwaves/Laser Technology
Product Engineering
Vertical World (The Magazine of Helicopters)

In addition to magazines specializing in specific technical fields, there are many others that may be of general interest to the engineer. They cover such fields as management, purchasing, and data processing.

*EDN,* put out by Cahners Publishing Company, is typical of the leading technical magazines. Its readership is made up of designers and design managers in electronics. Editor Glen Boe tells about the requirements and opportunities for writer/editors at *EDN:*

Being a printed medium for electronic engineers, we need a combination of both journalistic and technical talent. Because it is rare for beginning editors to have such a double background, our staff is composed of both journalists and engineers, each of whom contributes his own brand of know-how.

Today, the hallmark of a leading technical magazine is that synergistic combination of technical accuracy and timeliness, language that communicates in a lucid, fascinating way, and appealing graphics. As such, technical magazines need technical-minded journalists, communicative engineers, and graphic arts specialists at all levels.

Our need for breadth in both technical and geographic coverage gives rise to a broad range of jobs. We have several regional editors who cover specific geographic centers of industrial activity as well as copy editors and technical specialists at the home office. Travel budgets are liberal in order to keep us in intimate contact with the field we cover. Some publishers have regional news bureaus that write stories and gather information for several different magazines. There are also many opportunities for expanding into seminars, symposia, trade shows, audio-visual media, and books because our real business is communicating technical information—not just publishing magazines.

It is apparent from the above summary that the technical magazine field is a natural for the young person with a science or engineering degree, some ability in writing, and a little journalism experience, who wants the excitement of ranging broadly over his technical field (and perhaps equally broadly over the country) finding out the latest breakthroughs and reporting them to his engineering colleagues. This brand of technical writing requires expansive enthusiasm for the job and unlimited dedication to it, because it is as demanding as it is fun.

As you gain experience in this field, you can become the nation's expert in a given specialty; you know all the leading researchers in that area; you are able to write reflective, in-depth studies of the field as a whole; you are called automatically when a major breakthrough occurs. Those are some of the potential benefits of growing up with the technical magazine field; we do not want to suggest that it is fun only for the young. Rather the pervasive excitement of its working atmosphere makes it a field that many thrive on as a lifetime career.

*Scientific Professional Journals*

Virtually all basic scientific research results—the new discoveries about the nature of the world and the universe or about the properties of subatomic particles and of the practical compounds of commerce—all are reported to the scientific community through the authenticating medium of the scientific professional journal. Those journals publish articles written by researchers from across the country and around the world.

The bulk of the words that occur in such journals, therefore, originate with the scientists, not with the journal staff. Yet most require at least a modest paid staff of professional editors to accept articles, get them reviewed by experts in the field, do a light job of copy-editing, get the articles set in type, proofread them, send proofs to the author, evaluate the author's corrections, and see that he is properly charged for inserting new material.

To be adaptable to this kind of job, you must be good at English, competent in the science of the journal in question, and willing to spend the bulk of your time editing and processing with relatively few person-to-person professional contacts outside the office (most contacts with the scientist-authors are by letter only). This job is not as exciting as writing for a technical magazine, but it does keep you in touch with the leading edge of scientific research, and it does give you the psychic reward of knowing you have played an important part in disseminating scientific knowledge.

## Technical Books

Like the professional journals, technical books are sources of scientific and engineering information. Unlike journals, which present, for the most part, a random hodgepodge of new information, the technical book presents a consolidated, well-established body of information in an organized and structured way. Sometimes the structure is built around a well-confirmed theory. At other times—as in a handbook—it is structured in a purely arbitrary mechanical fashion to make it easy to find.

The book editor's job is at once less confining and in some ways more demanding than that of the journal editor. The book editor must know the technical fields he is dealing with in enough depth so that he understands which books will sell and which will not. He should get to know the leading figures in his technical fields, whether their books are published by his company or not. He must know who can write well enough to command an audience. He will often find that he is soliciting manuscripts and arranging contracts, thus functioning in much the same way as a salesman. And, of course, he must be personally a first-rate editor, as he must evaluate manuscripts, suggest to authors those areas that require rewriting, and often work with the authors to see that the changes are properly made. Persuading the author to make the changes you want is often far more difficult than just editing a manuscript yourself. It is a job that demands unfailing tact and unending patience, but it carries with it rich rewards of personal satisfaction.

## Technical Writing in the Biological Sciences

So far, in this chapter, our emphasis has been on the technical writing opportunities that are available in the physical sciences and engineering. That emphasis reflects the real world, because by far the largest proportion of technical writing jobs have been in the physical science and engineering areas.

But we would not be giving you a complete picture of the available opportunities if we neglected the technical writing that is done in support of the biological sciences and medicine.

### Medical Journal Editing

As is well known, physicians, surgeons, and medical researchers are studying diseases, the effects of foods and chemicals, new forms of medical treatment, and new surgical procedures. All that work must be reported to the medical profession in order to be useful. There are the general medical journals such as the *Journal of the American Medical Association* and the *Archives of Surgery*. But to serve the needs of the medical specialties, there are also journals of pediatrics, pharmacology, orthopedics, psychiatry, urology, cardiology, and many more.

The people who publish articles in such journals are physicians, surgeons, and medical researchers who, with few exceptions, write up their own work. Some draw their own illustrations as well. Some rely on photographs for illustrations. Others call on the services of medical illustrators—a select and highly skilled group whose profession was launched in this country largely through the teaching career of Max Broedel at The Johns Hopkins Medical School (see Fig. 10). Usually some of the same investigators serve from time to time as editors of the journals in their specialty, serving for a year or two at a time. A few of the journals, however, have full-time professional editors, and many others either have their own professional editors serving under the management of the rotating editor or have the editorial staff of a publishing house do most of the day-to-day editing work.

The job of those editors is much like that of the working editor in a scientific or engineering journal except that the specialized lan-

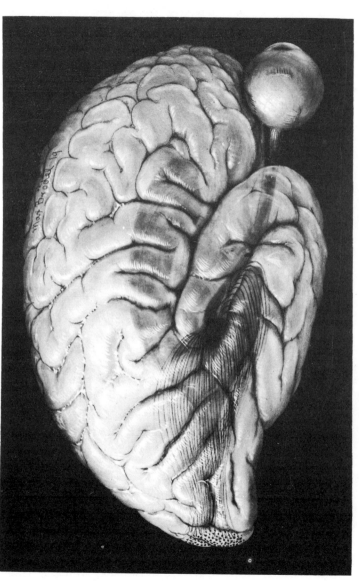

*Fig. 10. Medical writers rely upon illustrations to supplement their texts. Here is one by the master of medical illustration, Max Broedel.*

guage of the medical profession is quite different from that of the
physical scientist or engineer. The language of each is highly specialized—so much so that both are virtually incomprehensible to
the untutored layman. But they are also different from each other.
It is for that reason that we suggest that the technical writer—the
one who is going to be writing or editing material to be read and
used by specialists in the field—select either the physical sciences
or the biological sciences, but not try to combine both. To combine
them would be a little like a linguist whose native language was
English and who had mastered the Romance languages (French,
Italian, Spanish and Portuguese) deciding to add Swahili or Hindu-
stani to his repertoire—not impossible, but a tremendous challenge.

In addition to knowing the language of medicine, biology, and
physiology, the editor of a medical journal must be especially meticulous because errors can mean the difference between life and
death—in dosages, for example, a misplaced decimal point or an
erroneous unit of measure could be disastrous. Yet this career has
the special fascination of keeping you in the forefront of medical
knowledge and the unique satisfaction of knowing you are contributing to the saving of lives.

*Pharmaceutical Writing.* Virtually every manufacturer of pre-
scription drugs (pharmaceuticals) maintains a large staff of research
scientists whose job is to discover and develop new drugs to help
physicians in their continuing battle against disease. As they complete a research unit, they write it up either for publication in a professional journal or as a report for circulation within the pharmaceutical industry, or as a report to document their work for the benefit of other laboratory workers within the company.

Most such companies also employ writers to work with their scientists in preparing the articles and reports for publication. Those
men and women usually view themselves as "medical writers" rather
than "technical writers." (They think of "technical writers" as those
involved in the physical sciences and engineering.) But as we have
defined technical writers, pharmaceutical writers, who are writing
either for other researchers or for physicians and surgeons, are writing
for a technically trained audience rather than for the general public,
and so come under our general category of technical writers.

In describing the work of pharmaceutical writers, Frank T. Hess, who is in charge of medical writing for McNeil Laboratories, makes it clear that these men and women sometimes work as writers, sometimes as editors, in their handling of articles and reports:

> The medical writer may come in at any point in the preparation of a scientific report, starting with raw data and proceeding to tabulate, compare, analyze, and draw conclusions and commit these to paper. He may take a hopelessly confused and incomprehensible manuscript, and, by working with the original data, bring forth a usable report that makes some contribution to medical knowledge. In some instances he may need only suggest small changes in an already good paper. But with any project, no matter how near completion it may look when he takes it on, he must be ready to dig back down to the original work and start again.

But the writer in a pharmaceutical company is not limited to work on laboratory reports or journal articles. He has several other functions. As Hess describes, he

- helps prepare submissions to the FDA that summarize the results of preclinical and clinical investigations. In the final phase, the writer helps prepare the all-important New Drug Application made to the FDA.
- prepares the physician's brochure, which is a summary account of all biological work. It is continually supplemented with new information during the development cycle of the drug.
- helps the investigator prepare his "report of clinical findings," which may be presented as an article in a medical journal, as a paper at a scientific meeting, or as a scientific exhibit.
- prepares the package insert that tells the practicing physician what he needs to know about the drug's effectiveness and safety.

Those are the jobs of the pharmaceutical medical writer. But what kind of person is he? How does one prepare for such a job? And is the training so specialized that, once taken, your opportunities are severely limited? Hess addresses himself to those questions in the following paragraphs:

> What is the medical writer trying to do? Primarily he is trying to prepare an accurate, interesting report of an investigation. Accuracy is the ethical core of all of the writer's efforts. If he is not willing to sacrifice everything else to accuracy, the writer is in the wrong field. The next most important goal of the medical writer is interest. No matter what the importance of what he has to say, if it is not read, he has failed.

> There seems to be no single path leading to a career in medical writing. Nowadays, most medical writers are trained scientists who are particularly interested in the clear, accurate transmission of scientific information. But there are also effective medical writers whose training has not been scientific, but who are successful because they believe there should be a precise correspondence between an event and the description of it.

> More important than his specific training are the writer's attitudes toward his material. First, he must be unwilling to let any statement stand that is either inaccurate or unclear. Second, he must be alert enough to recognize when these conditions exist. Neither attitude is easy to develop, nor is either easy to live with when developed.

> The skills the pharmaceutical medical writer develops help prepare him for other science writing opportunities. For example, science writers are needed in textbook preparation, in medical and lay journalism, and in educational film and television writing. The need in these fields should increase, and many other fields will open up with time.

## Medical Electronics

The application of engineering, especially electronic engineering, techniques to solve medical problems is one of the major growth fields of this decade. It is predicted that by 1980, some $5,000,000,000 will be spent each year for electronics equipment in support of medicine.

Some applications of electronics to medicine have been used long enough to be familiar to the public: the X ray, the electrocardiograph, the electroencephalograph, the hearing aid, the intensive-care unit with its system of monitors (see Fig. 11), and the cardiac pacer probably sound familiar to most of you.

But the major challenge to be faced in this decade is the problem of the delivery of medical services. Not only are some communities entirely without medical care, but even in the cities, the patient load is overwhelming the available physicians and surgeons. As a result, the quality of medical care tends to go down as the doctor hurries from one patient to the next, the care available is misdirected as the doctor must spend as much time with patients whose symptoms are merely imagined as with the truly sick, and the cost tends to increase to the point that the poor cannot afford care at all.

One solution that has been suggested for the problem, and that has been tried successfully on a small scale, is a system of medical centers in which the patients are first screened by a broad-band series of laboratory and electronic tests and the results are fed at once into a computer that sorts out abnormal readings, suggests possible diagnoses, earmarks the seriously ill for the immediate attention of a physician, and recommends interim therapy for those with minor ailments. The tests, which can be conducted by medical technicians, combine with the computer analysis to allocate the time of the skilled physicians and surgeons where it is needed most.

Thus, a new career for writers is emerging, as electronics manufacturers will be needing writers who understand both the electronic equipment and the point of view of the physicians, who may need some persuasion to reach out and use some of the newer devices the biomedical development engineers are placing at their disposal.

Those writers are likely to be working at the report-article-brochure end of the technical writing spectrum. Most of them are likely to be already working in industry or a research laboratory and be asked to expand their scope to cover this new field. They are more likely to be drawn from those trained in the physical sciences than from those trained in the biological. But anyone who wants to train himself in this particular hybrid field will find increasing opportunities to use his dual talents.

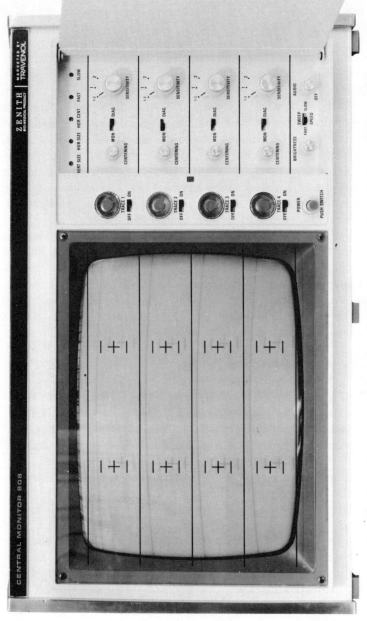

Fig. 11. *A medical electronics unit that displays simultaneously four different characteristics of the circulatory system.*

COURTESY ZENITH RADIO CORPORATION

*Agricultural Writing*

Not all biological writing has to do with medicine. The production of plants and animals for use as food is a vitally necessary part of our nation's life. Ways to improve the productivity of the soil and the quality of agricultural products are studied in the biological research laboratories of both the government and private industry. The government devotes most of its research to increasing the productivity of our farms; industry discovers ways to make the farmer's life easier and more efficient and to process, preserve, and distribute agricultural products most effectively.

Over the years, the U.S. Department of Agriculture has developed both a worldwide reputation for improving agricultural productivity and a highly effective system of disseminating that information to the nation's farmers. The Department's Office of Information uses many writers who are knowledgeable in the biological sciences. Dr. Robert B. Rathbone, its Director, explains how and why:

> In a nation where only about four percent of the people are farmers, it would appear that writing about the agricultural sciences offers, at best, only limited career opportunities.
>
> Not so. The farm population may be limited, but the sciences are not. In the U.S. there are perhaps as many as 20,000 scientists working with the plants, animals, soils, water, and air that constitute agriculture.
>
> These agricultural scientists do very practical research, such as breeding an oblong, tough-skinned (but tasty!) tomato that can be machine-harvested without bruising. But they also dig into the nature of viruses and try to understand the intricate relationships between light and life.
>
> The point is, there's no shortage of material here for the ambitious science writer; neither in scope nor depth. The agricultural sciences will continually challenge him to broaden his knowledge and improve his skills. And, as important as professional stimulation is, the agricultural sciences meet an even more basic incentive of all science writing: readership.
>
> To begin with, there are some people who must know what's

going on in the laboratories of the agricultural scientists. These are the nearly 3 million farmers—and additional tens of millions of people who have jobs related to agriculture—who absolutely depend on timely, responsible reporting. How else can they keep pace with an industry that serves the world as a model of successful scientific application?

Then, there are the urbanized Americans who need to know. Most of them will live out their lives without setting foot on a farm (let alone in the laboratory of an agricultural scientist), yet it is important that they at least know *about* the scientific goals and achievements of agriculture. It is important because the plants, animals, soils, water, and air that are the substances of the agricultural sciences translate into food, clothing, and homes. They are the raw materials of good nutrition, of environmental quality.

Americans need to know that food abundance and quality are, to a large extent, scientific payoffs and that today's research is determining how well some 266 million Americans will eat in the year 2000.

They need to know that conserving our natural resources is not a new idea to agricultural scientists, who have learned much about keeping our land productive. The patterns of conservation farming, so apparent to the air traveler, have application to urban and suburban land development and highway construction.

It is not enough for these people to recognize pesticides as a threat to the environment. They need to know that if enough food is to be produced without pesticides, agricultural science must find other ways to control pests and diseases that cost the economy an estimated $13 billion a year.

Obviously, the agricultural science writer is the bridge to farmers and non-farmers alike. Public understanding of these and other national issues depends on how well he makes the connections.

For his agricultural readers, the agricultural science writer must be informed, up to the minute, and lucid. For all the others, he must be meaningful; he must interpret, analyze, evaluate. He must put the agricultural sciences into the context of the non-agricultural world in which they work and live.

From that description, it is apparent that many agricultural writers straddle the dividing line between technical and science writers. They write for farmers—the agricultural specialists—but they also write for the general public. Thus, they need to be oriented toward the biological sciences, but they are not using as sophisticated a specialized vocabulary as are the medical or pharmaceutical writers. Their writing talents must be just as highly developed, however, for they must be able to write for the general public as well as for the agricultural specialist.

In the Department of Agriculture, writers prepare primarily information booklets, folders, data sheets, and press releases. To that array is added the occasional book or brochure. In industry, their work consists more of research reports, brochures, and, occasionally, advertising copy.

In industry, the agricultural writer appears more like a technical writer with biological subject matter. In the government, he appears more like a biologically oriented science writer, the subject of our next chapter.

# CHAPTER VI

# You May Be a Science Writer

"Science writing is writing about science, medicine, the environment, technology, public health, and any of a score of related topics, for a *general* audience. The writer uses technical words only when essential and carefully defines and describes them for the reader in a way he would not do if writing for a technical audience." That definition of science writing is the one provided by Henry Goodman of the Council for the Advancement of Science Writing.

## How Many People Do This?

Partly because of the greater difficulty of the task and partly because of the more limited employment opportunities in the field, there are far fewer science writers than there are technical writers. We estimate that they probably number less than 10 percent of the larger group. If our estimate of 25,000 technical writers is close to the mark, we are now saying that there are not more than 2,500 science writers.

The number of science writers is rather strictly a function of the public's interest in science. In the past quarter century it is clear that the public's interest in science has been thoroughly aroused. Before that, it was interested in a new cure in medicine, discovery of a new comet or galaxy, speculations about life on Mars, the invention and commercial development of the radio and the phonograph, but not much else. And for that, who needed a specialist? No one. And, indeed, twenty-five or thirty years ago only a few of the jobs we now call science-writing jobs existed. The science novel and science fiction were with us then, as were both popular factual books on science and science texts, but far fewer people wrote books of that sort then than do now. As for the other science-writing jobs we will mention, almost none had yet been thought necessary.

What of the future? The phenomenal increase in science-oriented employment, in the practical uses to which war-born technology was put, and in the rate of medical research progress, have all stimulated public interest in science. More recently the space program, with its weather and communications satellites, the race to the moon, and the prospect of really finding out about the "canals" on Mars, has whetted the public's appetite for science news until it seems second only to its appetite for the sports pages.

We have already noted, however, that the popularity of the space program is waning, that even the research and development part of the defense budget may face tough sledding in Congress, and that, as a result, the growth curve of the technical writing profession will flatten out for a few years of moderate rather than explosive growth. How will those events affect science writing? Will its growth be similarly slowed?

First, we must point out that the growth in science writing in the past quarter century has been nothing like the growth of technical writing. Although the bulk of occupations in that specialty have been created over the past twenty-five years, the total numbers have not been so great that the growth of science writing could be called anything more than orderly and moderate.

Second, there seems to be no lessening of public interest in science, even though some of that interest is rather more negative than positive. Since ultimately the solution of pollution problems will depend on scientific ingenuity, even public interest in pollution provides work for the science writer. Interest in astronomical discoveries remains high. The space program will continue at some level and will reach out to other planets at least with automatic sensing equipment if not with men. Medical research will continue to make advances about which the public will be eager to hear. And the atomic reactor program has become a center of controversy.

The future holds no dearth of work for the science writer, but the job opportunities remain rather limited, and in so small a field, large numbers of additional openings cannot be expected. Still, if moderate growth rates on the order of 2 to 3 percent per year were to hold until the year 2000, the number of science writers then might reach

5,000. This evaluation says that there will be opportunities for qualified young men and women to carve out careers for themselves in
science writing. So if this area is your heart's desire and if you
realistically appraise yourself as having the talent and personality
for this work, by all means prepare yourself for it, and set out to
make your mark!

*What Do Science Writers Do?*

By comparison with most technical writers, science writers spend
a much larger proportion of their time collecting their information
and doing their writing and much less time worrying about the me-
chanics of publication.

If he works for one of the current media such as newspapers, magazines, radio, or television, the science writer may spend much of his
time "where the action is" as an on-the-scene, real-time reporter.
When "the action" is not something spectacular such as a space shot,
but rather is a discovery made after years of painstaking research,
the science writer uses the interview to get his story.

On the other hand, if the science writer is producing a book, he
may do most of his research in the library. There he can sift through
what has been written in other books, in journal articles, and in
government reports, and pull together the information he needs to
write his book.

If he works in the public information field, he may spend a fair
proportion of his time reading through technical reports from his
research departments to determine which are practical enough to
condense in booklets for public reference and which are newsworthy
enough to prepare press releases about.

The other major part of the science writer's job is the writing
itself. For the most part, it is utilitarian writing plus personality. If
he works for current media, there may be little time for writing
between the event and the reporting of it. On television or radio, the
science "writer" may be reporting orally as the event occurs. For
those science writers the use of language, the injection of excitement
and personality, the awareness of the scientific background, and the
reporting of present happenings must all blend together into an in-
stantaneous, coherent, intelligible stream of science writing. The

newspaper writer has only a little more time, and the magazine writer enough for a couple of hasty rewrites.

The pamphleteer and news release writer sometimes have time to polish and refine their work through many rewritings and editings, but often they are called upon for press bulletins on such short notice that their first drafts must be acceptable. The book writer should have no pressure of time at all, but often the author is not a full-time author, but carries the responsibilities of a regular job. Having promised his publisher a manuscript by a specific deadline, he all too often finds that it reaches him before he is ready for it.

As a rule, however, when the science writer has collected his material and has written the best version he has time for, he is done. Other people worry about seeing that his material is transmitted or set in type, or typed and proofread, or recorded on video tape. The science writer is already off on his next assignment.

When you consider all the factors involved in most science writing —the pressure of time, the quality of the writing, the injection of interest, the retention of scientific accuracy, the simplification required for audience understanding, the breadth of topics covered— it is little wonder that science writers are considered an elite group— their performance justifies the reputation.

### What Do Science Writers Produce?

In attempting to categorize the various science writing occupations, it has seemed most reasonable to classify them by the products they produce.

### News Articles

Although the number of science writers is quite small, their influence is exceedingly widespread. As the public's interest in science has increased, newspapers, news magazines, and the broadcasting media have recognized that they need reporters who specialize in science just as much as they need reporters who specialize in sports, politics, or foreign affairs. Because the circulation of a newspaper or news magazine numbers in the hundreds of thousands, and because the broadcasting media reach into nearly every home and car in the nation, science writers exert a tremendous influence on popular opinion—they reach literally millions of people daily.

As a writer's audience and influence increase, so does his responsibility to that audience. Science news reporters, therefore, work under the same burden of responsibility to provide accurate, fair, impartial, objective information to the public as do all other journalists. But although they must stick to the facts and must try to present a balanced, unbiased interpretation of those facts, they also share the journalist's responsibility for seeking out, within the facts, those aspects that will be of particular interest to people, and highlighting them. In addition, as we have said, they must know how to inject their own personal flavor into their writing or speaking so that the result will heighten reader interest and enthusiasm.

Peter Reich, aviation/space editor for the newspaper *Chicago Today,* obviously loves his profession. Here is what he says about it:

A chance to be an eye-witness to history and to tell others about it, that's the great reward of being a newsman assigned to cover the space program. My work has enabled me to be on hand for most of the heart-pounding moments of the Space Age.

I was there when our first spaceman, Alan B. Shepard, rode his slim, white Chrysler Redstone rocket 115 miles above the earth on May 5, 1961.

I watched John Glenn thunder aloft on his pioneering orbital flight less than a year later.

And I felt the ground tremble from the awesome thrust of the mighty Saturn 5—a rocket as tall as the clock tower of Chicago's Wrigley Building—as it hurled the Apollo 11 moon astronauts Neil Armstrong, Buzz Aldrin, and Mike Collins toward their date with destiny.

Four days later, at the Manned Spacecraft Center in Houston, at 3:19 p.m. on Sunday, July 20, 1969, I heard the electrifying words that flashed across 240,000 miles of space from the moon to Earth:

"Tranquility Base here. The Eagle has landed."

Peter Reich has won nine major awards, including the nation's top awards for aerospace reporting in 1966 and for space writing in 1970. He leads an adventurous life. He has flown to the Navy's below-the-ice base at the South Pole; he was one of the first newsmen to fly through the sound barrier; he has experienced zero-gravity in the astronauts' training plane. He hopes to be the first newsman to fly into orbit, perhaps even to the moon.

The rewards of this career go to writers who can create audience understanding of new scientific advances while evoking in the reader's or listener's imagination their magic and excitement.

But although the science writer tries to capture and convey whatever glamour there may be in his subject, the job itself is not always glamorous. Space spectaculars don't happen every day, and more mundane developments have exciting implications that also need to be reported.

A contrasting perspective on the life of a science newsman is given by Arthur Snider, Science Editor of the *Chicago Daily News,* who has done and observed much reporting of medical news in the public press:

> It is probably simpler to indicate what a medical writer is not than what he is. He is not a doctor, a teacher, or a researcher. He is not interested in determining the molecular structure of insulin, but he is interested in telling people how the biological researcher did evolve the molecular structure of insulin.
>
> His news comes from many sources: conventions, meetings, lectures, press conferences, press releases, scientific journals, books, telephone calls, and from material assembled to fulfill assignments.
>
> Some of the work has an element of excitement, of glamour, but most of it is routine reportage of little events.
>
> The medical writer's tools are the tools of any news reporter; namely, questions: What are you doing? How are you doing it? Why are you doing it? What have you found out? How did you happen to undertake it? Is there a practical application?
>
> The medical writer is prodded by space limitations and by edi-

tion time. Within an hour, in 300 to 700 words, he must summon enough facts to give the story scientific validity, enough background to point up its importance, enough color to make it interesting, enough explanation to make it understandable, and the jet propulsion to get it into print before his competitors. It goes without saying that a medical story must be written simply. A story that is not understood is wasted space.

A good medical story should be a balanced account. It should not give false emphasis or engender false hopes. It should not prematurely promise a breakthrough. It should not obscure negative results. Whenever possible, the story should credit work that has gone before. It should not aggrandize the author.

Medical writing is not for those who dislike long hours of reading, who lack curiosity, or who insist on regular hours for meals, sleeping, and working. But it is a satisfying field for those who have sensitivity, feeling, and compassion for people. Success in medical writing is not the reward of inborn, artistic impulses or of flashes of inspiration. It is the reward of application. Good medical writing evolves from a fair average of good work, not from occasionally miraculous performances.

Becoming a good medical reporter requires a good newspaper reporting background, just as does becoming a Washington correspondent, a foreign correspondent, or a columnist. The basic job of being a reporter is foremost because the same skills that a reporter uses to ferret out news, to check his facts, to write in the space and time at his disposal, and to write clearly and accurately are the skills required to write a medical story.

And, finally, a medical writer must understand not only the facts and language of medicine but also the medical man—how he functions and how he thinks. The usual medical man is quite an ordinary person with ordinary human strengths and human weaknesses. He is most concerned about his reputation among his peers. He has spent a lifetime building his professional reputation, and he does not intend to have it destroyed by appearing to be a publicity-seeker.

Thus, the life of a science writer for the public news media is basically the everyday hard work of the journalist who works when the news happens, writes against press deadlines, and suffers the frustrations inherent in interviewing reluctant newsmakers. But whether the science writer specializes in space news or in medical news or covers it all, he has the continuing satisfaction of knowing that he is making a major contribution to public understanding of developments and issues that will affect all our lives and those of our children for years to come.

## Booklets, News Releases, Speeches

Every organization, whether it be a profit-making business or industry, a nonprofit research and development laboratory, a union, a professional society, or a department or agency of the government, recognizes the importance of keeping its name before the public. To some degree, the purpose is simply to build up a reservoir of public goodwill; to some degree, the purpose is to keep its name in the mind of potential buyers, sponsors, members, users, or employees. Specific efforts to sell or hire, of course, appear in the form of paid advertisements. But most organizations try to keep their name before the public through news items, or by having staff members make speeches, or by issuing brochures and booklets that are designed to inform the public rather than sell it something.

The people who prepare such informational materials are often called Public Information Officers. That title is specifically used in the federal government, and others comparable to it are used by other organizations.

The job of the public information officer is to channel information about the organization into the public media as "news" whenever possible. The job involves evaluating events within the organization for their newsworthiness, writing news releases and sending them to the most likely medium—newspapers, trade magazines, radio, or television. It can involve setting up news interviews with company officials or specialists, writing speeches or preparing statements for delivery at a press conference, writing and publishing booklets about the organization, and preparing motion pictures or videotape releases for use on TV news shows.

Whenever a public information officer works for a scientific, engineering, biological, or medical organization, his work is so deeply involved in the substance of science and technology that he qualifies as a science writer.

## Books

Science has brought forth many kinds of books, many of them written by men and women who make their living as science journalists or scientists.

*Science Books.* Some are factual books that tell a general audience about some aspect of science. Dave Dietz is Science Editor of the Scripps-Howard Newspapers. Here is what he says about his career as a writer of science books:

> My books have been a by-product of my newspaper work, strictly a matter of moonlighting. It requires a grim determination to give up the requisite number of evenings, Saturday afternoons, and Sunday mornings to turn out a book.
>
> I think that most science books, both popular and textbooks, are by-products of a regular career as a university professor, a research scientist or engineer, a newspaperman, or a magazine writer. My guess is that there are comparatively few full-time book writers in the science field.
>
> At the moment I am at work on my ninth book. I have written four books of popular science for adults and four for young people. The books for youngsters are easier to write and more fun. It is a mistake, however, to think that you write down to young people. You don't.
>
> My *All About Satellites and Space Ships* has sold 300,000 copies to date and is still selling. According to Random House, the publisher, it has been one of the most popular books ever published for young readers. If I may brag a little more, my books have been translated into 17 languages to date.

Asked to provide a sample of his writing that has particular significance, Dave supplied this excerpt from his book *Atomic Science, Bombs, and Power:*

Mankind stands at the crossroads today. One road leads to an ever increasing pace of the atomic armaments race. Its fearful end may be the total destruction of civilization. The other road leads to the peaceful application of atomic energy for the good of mankind. It promises to usher in the most glorious era in the history of the world, the Era of Atomic Energy. Which road will mankind take? [1]

Dave finishes by saying "I don't think we know the answer yet. But I am an optimist, and I hope for the best."

*Science Textbooks.* Some books are written to instruct young people about science. Here is how Larry McCombs, Managing Editor of the educational publishing firm CRM Books describes the task of the science education writer:

The job is essentially that of translating the ideas of scientists for an audience of nonscientists, of whatever age. It involves a great deal of reading, talking to scientists, use of a good writing style, and an ability to think of ways to communicate scientific ideas so they will be meaningful to the intended audience.

How your career as a science education writer might develop is told by Peter Saecker, mathematics and science manager for Science Research Associates (SRA), a firm that is widely known for its materials for primary and secondary education:

A beginning science editor at SRA would edit and write certain types of simple materials. As he demonstrates competence and advances to higher positions, he becomes more concerned with the development of content—deciding what should be included, working with the author, and editing more complex materials. At higher levels, the editor will become a manager, planning and directing the work of others. As an editor, he may also do a major portion of the writing of a program, using outsiders as consultants rather than authors. This requires considerable ex-

---

[1] David Dietz, *Atomic Science, Bombs, and Power* (New York: Dodd, Mead & Co., 1954).

pertise in curriculum development, teaching methods, and subject matter, in addition to skills in writing, editing, and production.

Some books are written primarily to entertain, but draw heavily on scientific and quasi-scientific data, principles, or speculations. Often they use the technique of projecting the fictional events of the book into the future far enough to permit vast technological and scientific advances to have taken place, and then telling a story in that future context. The books fall into two broad categories—science fiction (which is often concerned with the fantastic adventures of a few Earthlings on a distant planet) and the science novel (which is usually concerned with possible future happenings here on Earth).

*Science Fiction.* Typical early writers of science fiction were Jules Verne (*From the Earth to the Moon*) and H. G. Wells (*The Time Machine* and *The War of the Worlds*). After that brilliant start, science fiction went downhill under the influence of the BEM (bug-eyed monster) school of science-fiction writing, in which the departures from the realm of scientific possibility became extreme.

But sprinkled in among the BEM-school offerings, there were a few, originally obscure, writers who predicted with uncanny and detailed accuracy a train of events that actually took place—the development of the atomic bomb, the moon voyage and landing, and the deep probes into space, together with many other feats yet to be accomplished but now well within the realm of possibility. Those obscure writers turned out to be such people as Isaac Asimov, Ray Bradbury, Robert A. Heinlein, and Arthur C. Clarke. They also turned out to have a devoted readership of distinguished scientists, some of whom had been influenced to take up their professions through their love of this type of science fiction.

In recent years, the better type of science fiction has reached a far wider audience through television and the motion picture. Gene Roddenberry's well-researched TV series *Star Trek* and Arthur C. Clarke's motion picture *2001: A Space Odyssey* are examples.

It's an exciting career, this writing of science fiction, and one capable of considerable growth. It requires imagination, the ability to write creatively, and most important, a sound basis of scientific and technical knowledge to lend that touch of credibility that makes it all believable.

*Science Novels.* Two examples of the science novel are *Brave New World* by Aldous Huxley, and *1984* by George Orwell. Both have had a profound impact upon our society and may well have influenced the course of history. Huxley describes an institution in which society is scientifically stratified, babies are decanted from bottles, and all are conditioned to live in perfect harmony. Orwell's *1984* is the pathetic story of the attempt of a man and woman to gain freedom from a stifling dictatorship in which thought as well as action is controlled.

The art of the novelist breathes the tension of life into his sociological commentary. Huxley, for example, describes the appearance and feelings of one of the denizens of the brave new world who had been scientifically stunted and conditioned to accept his lot without hope or recourse:

Before Bernard could answer, the lift came to a standstill.

"Roof!" called a creaking voice.

The liftman was a small simian creature, dressed in the black tunic of an Epsilon-Minus Semi-Moron.

"Roof!"

He flung open the gates. The warm glory of afternoon sunlight made him start and blink his eyes. "Oh, roof!" he repeated in a voice of rapture. He was as though suddenly and joyfully awakened from a dark and annihilating stupor. "Roof!"

He smiled up with a kind of doggily expectant adoration into the faces of his passengers. Talking and laughing together, they stepped out into the light. The liftman looked after them. "Roof?" he said once more, questioningly.

Then a bell rang, and from the ceiling of the lift a loud speaker began, very softly and yet very imperiously, to issue its commands.

"Go down," it said, "go down. Floor Eighteen. Go down, go down. Floor Eighteen. Go down, go . . ." The liftman slammed the gates, touched a button and instantly dropped back into the droning twilight of the well, the twilight of his own habitual stupor.[2]

Then, too, there are novelists who, though not science writers, weave science themes into their stories. John Updike is one of those. In *The Centaur,* his leading character, a high-school teacher named Caldwell, relates the age of the universe—5,000,000,000 years—to the span of man's time on earth. Using a scale of three days, Caldwell tells of the formation of the earth on Monday noon, then reviews the creation and evolution of life on ensuing days. As the noon dismissal bell rings on Thursday, Caldwell completes his story:

"One minute ago, flint-chipping, fire-kindling, death-foreseeing, a tragic animal appeared—" The buzzer rasped; halls rumbled throughout the vast building; faintness swooped at Caldwell but he held himself upright, having vowed to finish. "—called Man." [3]

To undertake science fiction or the science novel, a writer must be genuinely creative. The creative writer uses material other people know, but by the way he molds and shapes and phrases it, he creates something they did not know—a new idea, a new perspective. The source of creativity is a mystery. It probably lies buried deep in the subconscious mind—a wellspring that bubbles forth without conscious effort, scarcely under conscious control. Wherever it lies, however we come by it, have it we must to be a fiction writer; in this field the special magic achieved by creativity is essential.

*Audio-Visual Scripts.* Our last science-writing career is also the newest. It's a brand new field, and one with great career potential,

---

[2] Aldous Huxley, *Brave New World* (New York: Harper & Row, Publishers, Inc., copyright 1932, 1960 by Aldous Huxley), excerpt from pp. 69–70 reprinted by permission of the publisher.
[3] John Updike, *The Centaur* (New York: Alfred A. Knopf, Inc., 1957).

the writing of audio-visual scripts about science for educational television.

The basic requisites for this career are the same as those for the science education writer, but to them the TV script writer must add the mystery of a new medium. Because television is an *electronic* medium it puts at the writer's command an immense repertoire of auditory and visual effects that can greatly enhance message effectiveness—provided they are properly used! Learning how to use those effects is the primary challenge of this new field, and it can occur only on the job.

Dan Q. Posin is a writer who has won six Emmy awards as the Best Educator on TV. He writes his own material and also presents it on the screen. Since 1954, he has prepared nearly 1,500 programs on such topics as *Great Men in Science* and *What's New in Science.* The programs have appeared on NET—National Educational Television—and on local television stations in major cities.

A good part of Dr. Posin's success has been the result of his ability to match his science topics to the television medium, making them not only informative, but interesting and exciting as well.

Dr. Posin is not, strictly speaking, a professional science writer. He is Professor of Physical Sciences and Chairman of the Department of Interdisciplinary Sciences at San Francisco State College. In addition to his TV work, he has written twenty-four books.

Although Dr. Posin has not worked only in the television medium, he is still in a position to give good advice to those who might wish to make science education through television a career:

I believe that the future for science writing in television is very bright, except that it apparently takes great persistence, and often some influence for a young writer to make proper contacts. The greatest opportunities probably lie in TV shows on commercial stations, where actors are employed to portray the role of scientists. In educational television, the scientists, usually university professors, prefer to write their own material; preparation of detailed scripts is not necessary for them since they prefer to talk off the cuff for the whole program, following a simple outline. That is why I say that the best opportunities for science writers lie in the area of commercial shows where the actor does not need to know much about science.

As John Gardner has said: "The pieces of the educational revolution are lying around unassembled." Television is one of those pieces. Those who go into this field will themselves be the pioneers, building upon the examples of the Dan Q. Posins who have demonstrated the great potential of this medium for education.

# CHAPTER VII

## *Especially for the Ladies*

Technical and science writing are careers to which women should give particular consideration. Women, more often than men, are likely to have several major talents or interests, sometimes related, sometimes quite diverse. As we have seen, technical and science writing require a combination of diverse skills and interests—writing ability and an interest in language combined with considerable knowledge of, and interest in, the physical or biological sciences. That combination of talents is thus more likely to be found in a woman than a man, which helps to account for the fact that there are a large number of successful women technical writers and some women science writers.

Unfortunately, that happy combination of talents is not the only, perhaps not even the major, reason so many women have had careers in technical writing. Too often, women who have graduated from college with degrees in science or engineering have found no jobs open to them in research or in development. Too often, women who have started "line" careers in science or engineering have come to see that advancement opportunities into line supervisory positions or senior line grades were going only to men, perhaps men with lesser qualifications.

Faced with such inequitable treatment in line positions, many women, who saw that they also possessed writing capabilities, switched into the technical writing field in hope of better treatment, more variety and responsibility on the job, and even some realistic opportunities for individual growth, recognition, and advancement. For some, the switch worked, but not for all. In some companies, the lot of the woman technical writer is no better than that of the woman engineer or chemist, but in others, the opportunities for recognition and advancement have been significantly better in technical writing than in engineering or science.

With the new emphasis on truly equitable treatment for women that has recently come to the fore, it is earnestly to be hoped that in the years to come those women who want line careers in science and engineering will be able to take their rightful places beside men working in those fields. It should not again be necessary for a woman to enter technical writing as second best to engineering.

But just as there are some men who have that particular combination of talents and interests that points to a career combining writing and science, so some women have the same combination of skills and interests. For them, technical and science writing prove to be careers in which women can find not only ready acceptance because of the success of those who have preceded them but also opportunities to rise to positions of leadership.

An example is Mary M. Schaefer who was recently president of the Society for Technical Communication. She supervises the report writing and production staff of the Space Development Department at The Johns Hopkins University's Applied Physics Laboratory (see Fig. 12).

She was one of the pioneer women in the field; she was the first woman hired by the Maintenance Division of the Army Ordnance Department to edit technical manuals. Since then she has written and edited reports and manuals on mines, torpedoes, guided missile systems, and satellites.

She knows that men often express surprise at a woman's being able to understand something as complicated as a gun. She has often heard such comments as, "Why, my wife doesn't even know what a wrench is." But she knows, as do many other women and an increasing number of men, that, given the opportunity, women can understand mathematics, science, and engineering as well as men. In the early days, however, acceptance was nip and tuck. As Mary puts it:

Our supervisors observed our working habits very closely and thoroughly checked the quality and accuracy of our editing. Later I heard via the grapevine that my work compared favor-

*Fig. 12. Mary Schaefer, pioneer among women technical writers, advises a member of her staff.* COURTESY THE APPLIED PHYSICS LABORATORY OF THE JOHNS HOPKINS UNIVERSITY

ably with that of the men editors and was even better than that
of some of them, much to the satisfaction of the civilian head of
our Branch who had held out for hiring women editors, and
somewhat to the chagrin of his assistant who had not wanted to
hire women.

Mary's view of the situation at present is that:

A woman, by and large, must still prove herself, and in doing
so, she will often have to work harder than her male counter-
parts and yet receive a lower salary.

Nevertheless, she likes the technical writing field, for she says:

My career in technical communication has been stimulating; it
has put me in the vanguard of history; it presents an exciting
challenge, and more and more women are accepting that challenge.

A more recent (1968) graduate, Marthe E. Harwell, who prepared herself for technical writing by combining an English major
with a wide variety of science courses, found considerable difficulty
in locating her first job.
She was finally hired by a writing agency. She found that organization an excellent place to begin because:

I learned a wide range of skills—abstracting, the complete process of editing a manuscript, having it set into cold type, even
how to lay out pages of type and check the final copy that was
going to the printer.

She found it "a place of limited growth," however, and now is an
Editorial Assistant for the Highway Research Board of the National
Academy of Sciences. When asked if she thought that technical writ-
ing and editing are good careers for women, she says:

I can respond immediately with an emphatic "Yes!"

But then she adds quickly:

> All careers can be good for both men and women. I would like
> to see more young *men and women* made aware of the field of
> technical communication.

# CHAPTER VIII

## Preparing Yourself

. . . I grew up in the little town of Wasco, California . . . loved to read and write from an early age, and worked on school papers. As statistician for the school teams, I became a sports reporter for the local weekly newspaper . . . loved science in high school, and went to Caltech with the intention of becoming a chemist. Soon I discovered that research wasn't to my taste— I like communicating with people more than searching out new knowledge.

So wrote Larry McCombs, telling how he learned his profession of science writing. Two key factors weave through Larry's account— factors largely typical of all technical and science writers. First, a love of a field—science, in Larry's case; and second, a desire to *tell about it,* rather than just "do it."

It is an unusual combining of a knowledge and a skill, but it is typical of technical and science writers. Most students will select a career either in science or in communication, but not a combination of the two. That duality of interest makes the profession out of the ordinary; so it follows that school curricula leading to such a career are also rather uncommon. Unlike the student who wants to be a doctor, an engineer, or a physicist, you will not find a ready-made, time-tested curriculum awaiting you in the catalog of just any college or university you select.

Although a few universities have pioneered in setting up curricula for technical and science writers, unless you can attend one of those few schools, you will have to plan your own course of studies, taking a single course here and a string of others there—all directed toward the goal of learning the fundamentals of science—physical or biological as you prefer—and of learning how to write well, easily, quickly, and flexibly.

But planning your own curriculum is not all bad, for there is a certain excitement, exhilaration, and freedom in striking out on your own. Advisers are becoming more liberal in their approach to such multidisciplinary programs these days, but yours will probably still require you to pick a major: If you see yourself headed for technical writing, pick a science or engineering major; if you prefer science writing, your major should be in journalism with a strong science minor.

Before going further into this matter of education, let us review the requisites for the education of a technical and science writer, as set forth in previous chapters. Those requisites are summarized in Table I.

*Table I*

EDUCATIONAL REQUISITES FOR A CAREER
IN TECHNICAL OR SCIENCE WRITING

A. *Technical Knowledge* (Emphasis here for Technical Writers)
  1. Knowledge of fundamental principles of:
     a. Physical sciences (physics, chemistry), *or*
     b. Biological sciences (biology, physiology), *or*
     c. Engineering (aeronautical, electrical, electronic, mechanical, industrial [civil is less useful]). (Note that engineering is built on the principles of physics and chemistry, which are usually required early in an engineering program.), *or*
     d. Medicine (anatomy, physiology, etc., built on principles of biology and chemistry).
  2. Knowledge of basic mathematics (algebra, geometry, trigonometry, differential and integral calculus). (This item is especially important for those specializing in the physical sciences or engineering.)
  3. Knowledge of basic scientific methods (deductive logic, inductive logic, hypothetical reasoning, controlled experimentation, logic of confirmation). (Although this infor-

mation can be deduced from science courses, it is often
best obtained from a course in the philosophy of science
given in the philosophy department.)

B. *Writing Skill* (Emphasis here for Science Writers)

    1. Ability to organize information into logical sequences for effective presentation.

    2. Ability to use words and the grammatical structures of language accurately and precisely to convey exactly the desired meaning and feeling.

    3. Ability to write effectively for various types of audience.

    4. Ability to use language to achieve light, easy, uncluttered communication.

C. *Supporting Skill and Knowledge Areas*

    1. Touch typewriting (essential).

    2. Principles of diplomacy (getting along with other people) (essential).

    3. Principles of: (desirable, but can be learned on job)

       a. Good graphic design

       b. Types and uses of illustration

       c. Techniques of illustration, photography, reproduction, and printing.

    4. Principles and techniques of good supervision and management (desirable, but *can* be learned when needed).

D. *Personal Characteristics*

If you want to be a technical or science writer, use the period of your formal education to become aware of and develop in yourself these characteristics:

    1. Self-motivation (You want to do the work.)

    2. Self-discipline (You force yourself to do the work even when you don't really want to.)

    3. Self-management (You organize your time to get the work done.)

    4. Self-control (You always find ways to work pleasantly with others.)

    5. Precision (You want everything to be just right, but unlike the perfectionist, you recognize that most finished jobs contain minor flaws.)

6. Adaptability (You are willing to do the job the way somebody else thinks it should be done.)
7. Aptness (You learn many kinds of things quickly.)
8. Courage (You are willing, on occasion, to stick your neck out and stand up for a principle you believe in.)

## Sources of Education

Your education should start early as your interest in things scientific and technical is sparked at the elementary level. In high school, you can begin to build a sound foundation in science and can begin to find out whether you prefer the physical or biological sciences by taking courses in biology, chemistry, physics, and mathematics. Your courses in English will also be starting you on the road to skillful use of language. In many localities, other essential skills such as typing and photography can be acquired at the high-school level.

Practical experience can be gained in off-hours and summers by working on school publications, or in a local newspaper or print-shop.

Beyond high school? You may have a chance to go on to college. If so, take it, as every additional bit of education you can get will be beneficial, no matter what career you select. At present, unfortunately, college and university curricula specifically designed to prepare you for a career in technical writing or in science writing are relatively rare.

## College-level courses

Despite their rarity, a few universities have such curricula, notably, the women's college of the Carnegie Institute of Technology in Pittsburgh, Colorado State University in Fort Collins, Iowa State University of Science and Technology in Ames, the University of Missouri in Columbia, and Arizona State University at Tempe. Most of the programs, however, are sponsored by the English or Journalism Departments and so are relatively weak in the scientific component of their curricula. In addition, two colleges offer graduate-degree programs in writing for undergraduate science, engineering, and mathematics majors. The program at Rensselaer Polytechnic Institute (RPI) in Troy, New York, prepares its graduates for careers in technical writing. The program at Boston University's School of Public Communication prepares its graduates for careers as science writers.

If you are not able to attend one of those schools, you will probably be able to devise a program that will give you the two prime tools—scientific knowledge and writing skill—in the proportions you will need. To do so, you will have to take what the schools call an "interdisciplinary" program. In the past ten years, it has become a lot easier to take an interdisciplinary program than it used to be, but our advice is for you to read college catalogs carefully to see what curricula are already available and to see what attitude the schools take toward interdisciplinary programs. (Even if you want to try to attend one of the schools mentioned above, get its catalog first to make sure its curriculum suits your interests.)

Let us look at various ways you might build an interdisciplinary program.

If you are primarily interested in technical writing, you will want to place major emphasis on the science-knowledge tool. To do so, you might:

1. Take a college major in physics, chemistry, biology, or any branch of engineering (except civil).
   Advantages: • Gain in-depth knowledge of one field.
   • Have job possibilities in field itself.
   • Can go to graduate school in your major.
   Disadvantage: • Curriculum too full to add many writing courses.
2. Take a college major in industrial engineering, industrial management or engineering management.
   Advantages: • Gain broad survey of math, science, engineering without going into any area in depth.
   • Learn management skills such as programming, scheduling, accounting, decision-making.
   • Have opportunities in careers such as sales, public relations, advertising, personnel.

Disadvantage: • Curriculum too full to add many writing courses.

*NOTE:* RPI's graduate writing program leading to a master's degree overcomes the above disadvantage, but takes another year.

If you are primarily interested in science writing, you will want to place major emphasis on the writing-skill tool. In that case, you might:

1. Take a college major in journalism with a minor in science.
   Advantages: • Learn the basics of journalism.
   • Prepare for beginning journalism jobs.
   • Curriculum can accommodate a minor.
   Disadvantage: • May have difficulty taking a broad enough range of science courses.

2. If your college lacks a journalism department, take a major in English and a minor in science.
   Advantages: • Gain more background in literature.
   • Curriculum can accommodate a minor.
   Disadvantages: • Have less writing practice.
   • May have difficulty taking a broad enough range of science courses.
   • Have less awareness of journalistic practices.

On the other hand, you may not be interested in as broad an educational program as most colleges provide, or your grades may not be quite good enough for admission to college, or you may not be able to attend college for financial reasons. If you are interested in a career in technical writing, particularly electronics writing, you might:

1. Attend a technical or trade school for training as an electronic technician.
   Advantages: • Learn a trade.
   • Concentrate in one specialty.
   • Save time compared to college.
   • Save money compared to college.

Disadvantages:  • Must learn writing on your own.
                       • Have less growth potential than with college training.

2. Volunteer for one of the military services with, if possible, preenlistment guarantee of electronic technician training.

Advantages:  • Learn a trade.
                  • Concentrate in one specialty.
                  • Training takes less time than college.
                  • Training is free.
                  • You get work experience in field.

Disadvantages:  • Must learn writing on your own.
                       • Have less growth potential than with college training.

A final word needs to be added about learning writing skill. In elementary and high school you learn—or should learn—the basics of grammar, spelling, and punctuation. (For later reference, the same material is in most dictionaries.) Knowing the basics is not enough, however; you must practice! Ideally, you should practice where your writing will be criticized and corrected, where someone will guide you toward more fluent modes of expression.

If you go to college you may find people to help you with your writing:

- in the journalism department.
- in the English department.
- even in some engineering or science departments.
- on the staff of the college newspaper.
- on the staff of the college yearbook.
- in the literature, creative writing, or debating clubs.
- on the staff of the college radio station.

If you think you may not get to college, even during high school or in the service, you may be able to acquire some guided writing experience in such activities as these:

- Work on the school newspaper or yearbook.
- Part-time work for a weekly newspaper.

- Participation in English or debating clubs.
- Work on a post newspaper.

However you go about preparing for your career in technical and science writing, do not be afraid to ask for help. If you ask often enough, the chances are good that someone will be eager to lend a hand.

Here, for example, is what Professor Ben H. Baldwin of Northwestern University's Medill School says:

. . . when I find a student who is particularly interested in science writing, I can help him put together a broadly based program which leads him into various scientific disciplines within the University. I can sometimes put together a special program for him including independent studies, etc., which would relate to his special interests.

After your initial spurt of higher education, you may wish you knew more in some area. Remember that other educational opportunities are readily available—for example:

- Short college extension courses in special subjects.
- Seminars and symposia sponsored by professional associations.
- Company sponsored courses.
- Evening courses offered by high schools and colleges.

How much education you will need depends on the type of work you will do. But whatever aspect of technical or science writing you go into, it is helpful to get as much education as you can. The scope of your career and how far you can go in this (or any) profession is pretty much a function of how much usable education you have.

*An Imperative—"Continuing Education"*

Besides having a revolutionary effect on society, the "information explosion" has yet another effect—it renders the knowledge of engineers and scientists obsolete at an alarming rate. For example, one half of an engineer's education is said to be obsolete seven years after his graduation. As a result, according to the National Science Foundation, engineers and scientists spend at least ten hours a week in work-related reading, plus forty to fifty hours a year in special courses of study.

Technical and science writers are in the same boat, with a plus (or is it a minus?) added. Not only does the writer's knowledge of science and technology become obsolete, but so does his other basic knowledge requisite—communication—in which the changes are even more rapid and revolutionary.

As with engineers and scientists, the writer's solution is a program of "continuing education"—an education that must be carried on throughout his professional lifetime. As with engineers and scientists, it consists of a personal program of reading of technical and scientific literature, and the literature on communication as found in trade magazines and professional periodicals. Attendance at university extension courses and at the conferences, seminars, and symposia sponsored by professional associations is also necessary.

But continuing education is no drag: For one thing, *all* professionals—doctors, lawyers, managers—must continue their education and must do it outside their normal working hours. And there is a compensation—as your field renews itself through new discoveries, so will your interest be renewed.

So, in this profession, education, like gold, is where you find it. But there are many sources, many places, many ways to gain an education in technical and science writing. The ultimate requisite for any program of learning is an inquiring, restless mind—a mind alert to see what is good and usable, coupled with an urge (as a true writer) to tell about it in new, interesting ways.

That is what makes this profession particularly meaningful, and that is what makes it fun.

# CHAPTER IX

# Getting That Job

The time will soon come to put your education to practical use and to get a return on the investment of time and money that you represent—in short, the time will come to get a job.

The words that follow on the subject are going to be utterly practical. Too many inexperienced young people seek jobs in a haphazard fashion, with the result that they "fall into" the first job that comes their way. If they are lucky, the spot they fall into may be reasonably good for them; if not, they may get trapped into a permanent dead end that will sap their ambition and pay them but a fraction of what their talents might otherwise have earned them.

Obviously, this matter of job-seeking is much too important to leave to luck. You should become an expert in how to find a job for *you*. No subject is more worthy of study.

The sections that follow are tailored to finding jobs in the technical and science writing fields. Much more in general can be said; your school guidance or placement office, your school library, and the public libraries can supply you with books and pamphlets on how to prepare for and find jobs. Add some of them to your reading list.

## Job-Locating Techniques

How do you become aware of a job that fits your potential?

Employers must let people know that they need certain services. They do so in four basic ways:

- Through your school's placement office
- Through advertising

- Through professional associations
- Through employment agencies

*Placement Office.* Virtually every college and university of any size, and many junior colleges and technical schools, maintain full-time placement offices on campus. Business, industrial, government, and research and development organizations—all the sorts of places you might want to work—send brochures, booklets, and folders full of leaflets to those placement offices. Such company literature is usually displayed on racks, and you are welcome to come in and browse.

The company booklets usually tell a little about the company, its history, its objectives, its products. They indicate what kinds of people the company needs to hire, and they often tell what employees with various backgrounds do on the job. The booklets also tell where the company is, what kind of climate is found there, what universities are nearby in case you want to do graduate work, and describe the local community.

But the companies do more than send booklets. Each year each one sends a personnel representative to dozens of colleges and universities. He tells your school's placement officer when he is coming and asks him to set up appointments for him with seniors who might be interested in that company. That way, you will have ample opportunity to talk to several employer representatives during your senior year and may be well on your way to having a job before graduation. Probably close to 80 percent of all college graduates now get their first job as a result of a contact made through the placement office.

As we have said all along, however, technical writing and science writing are unusual. Because they do not fit the usual categories, you may find it particularly helpful to discuss with your placement officer where you might find opportunities best suited to your job goals.

*Advertising.* If the placement office offers few prospects, if your school has no placement office, or if you are not affiliated with a school when you are seeking a job, you may want to work through advertisements. Employers advertise specific positions they have open, but you need to know where to look for the ads.

If you want a job in one particular city or in a particular part of the country, you will be most likely to find the jobs you want advertised in the major newspapers serving that part of the country. If you do not care about location but want to search the country as a whole, your best bet is to buy a *New York Times* for several Sundays.

With newspaper in hand, you seek out the "classified" pages in which job openings are advertised. The openings are listed alphabetically by job title. If you want to be a technical writer or editor, that is the job title most frequently used, but you will sometimes find jobs listed under the other technical writing job titles given in Chapter V. If you want to be a science writer, you will, to start, just be looking for a job as a newspaper reporter or journalist.

You should also look for ads in the trade magazines. Especially if you hope to be a technical writer and have specialized in one area of science or technology, check the trade journals that serve that technical area. Very often companies advertise for writers and editors in the same journals they use to seek their technical staff because they want people with the same technical background.

When you find an ad that interests you, send off your résumé with a cover letter to apply for the job.

*Professional Associations.* You will want to join a professional association as an aid to your own professional growth. Many associations (both in technical or scientific specialties and in technical or science writing) help their members find jobs. They run ads by employers in their journals. Sometimes they keep local logs of available jobs. Sometimes they keep rosters of résumés of available members. Association members in supervisory positions often support the association by seeking employees from among the members before turning to other sources.

*Employment Agencies.* For a fee, which is usually paid by the employer, an employment agency will try to match candidates to jobs. Probably because of the success of the college placement offices, relatively few college graduates use agencies to find their first job; but there is no reason not to use an agency if it appears to be a wise move in your specific situation.

An agency can be very helpful in giving advice on the state of the job market and on how to prepare your résumé. In fact, some agencies will prepare your résumé for you.

Save yourself from embarrassment by checking out the agency before you go into it. Some agencies specialize in secretarial and clerical placements exclusively, whereas others emphasize professional placements. Obviously, you want the latter type. Do not be surprised, either, if an agency says it does not think it can help you. That just means they do not have the right contacts for your type of job. By sending you away, they are doing you a favor, because you will not be wasting time on a contact that will not get results. Keep looking! You'll find one that can help you.

**However you decide to make contact with a potential employer, remember this: The placement office, advertisement, professional society, and employment agency provide you only with initial contacts. Once you meet an employer's representative, you, and you alone, must sell yourself. You must impress that representative (and usually the supervisor for whom you will work) with your competence, eagerness, friendliness, and self-assurance. If you don't think you can do the job, nobody else will!**

*"Writing Your Ticket"—the Résumé*

The résumé is a written summary of your training, experience, and capabilities. It provides the prospective employer with a capsule description of what you have to offer. If he likes what he reads and if it is relevant to his needs, he will contact you for an interview.

So the résumé is a sales tool. It is much like the brochure that sells a product; but in this case *you* are the product. Like the brochure, your résumé is the first glimpse of you that a prospective employer will get. Unless it is a good résumé, it will be *all* he'll see of you! So it is vitally important for you to make absolutely sure that your résumé is flawless.

As you set about preparing your first résumé, you may think you have little to offer an employer. But do not downgrade yourself— think positively! You have your youth, your eagerness, your ambition, your training, and your willingness to work. Remember, the employer who is looking for a new graduate expects to spend some months providing you with additional training about his jobs, his plant, his products. The faster you learn and become productive, the more valuable you become to him.

So, in putting your résumé together, think of all the things you have done that might help persuade an employer to take a closer look at you. Don't be bashful!

All right, now, are you in the proper frame of mind? OK, let's write.

1. *Your Name, Address, and Telephone Number.* If the company can't reach you, you're dead! If you are at school but will be leaving soon (or even going home on vacation), put down both your school address and a permanent address through which you can always be reached. Be sure your address includes your Zip Code. Be sure your telephone number includes your area code.

2. *Your Career Objective.* The point of this section is to let the employer know that you know where you are headed. In general, an employer prefers a person with a specific goal to one who is willing to drift into anything that comes along. State your career objective simply and matter-of-factly; avoid grandiose statements that are not in keeping with your training and experience. Here are a couple of examples: "I want to write technical manuals in the electronics field." "I want to become a newspaper reporter and work toward becoming a science writer."

3. *Your Education.* Starting with high school, list all the technical, trade, and service schools you have attended, the junior colleges, colleges, and universities. With the name and location of each one, list the dates you attended, your major subject of study, and any certificate or degree you received. Include special short courses, summer courses, symposia, and workshops.

4. *Your Experience.* Here your prospective employer is interested primarily in *relevant* experience. You can safely omit the summer you spent selling shoes or working in a plumbing-supply house. But if you have spent summers working for a local weekly newspaper, or in a printshop, or as a proofreader, put that down. If you have worked on school newspapers, magazines, yearbooks, or radio stations, include that information. If you have been a member of literary, science, debating, or photographic clubs at school or in the community, be sure to mention them. Your experience listing should include names of the organizations for which you worked, their addresses, the dates you worked for or were a member of them, the title of your position, and a brief summary of the type of work you did in that position.

5. *Your Professional Society Memberships.* Even as a student you may have become aware of various professional associations, as many of them maintain active student chapters on campuses across the country. If you have joined one or more such professional associations, list them, and the date-span of your membership. If you belong to special-interest groups within an association, note them. If you have served as an officer of a student chapter, note that, too.

6. *Special Achievements.* This is a catch-all category for things you think an employer might want to know about you that do not fit in the earlier categories. Put here such things as National Merit Scholarships; special college or university scholarships and fellowships; academic honors, awards, and prizes; academic offices held; honor society memberships; published articles; papers presented at professional society meetings; and so on.

7. *References.* Sooner or later each employer you contact will ask you for references, that is, for the names, addresses, and telephone numbers of people who know you, your character, and your professional capabilities. So you might as well collect the information you need right at the beginning and put it in your résumé. The chairman of your major department, a faculty adviser to the student paper, your immediate supervisor at the weekly paper you worked for last summer—these are examples of the type of people the employers will want to contact. Before listing a person as a reference, however, you should ask him if you may do so, so he will be prepared to receive calls about you.

8. *Personal Facts.* Usually an employer likes to know your height, weight, and marital status.

Those are the facts you need to present in your résumé. How they are presented—that is, how they are organized and arranged on the page—is called formatting. Formatting is an important part of résumé preparation. It makes a difference both to the initial impression your résumé makes and to its readability.

Your objective in formatting is to present a page of information (try to keep it to one page) that is pleasing to the eye, that is easy to read, and that is arranged in a logical and consistent manner. Here are some formatting guidelines that will help:

- Center your material on the page side-to-side and top-to-bottom.
- Use wide margins (1 to 1½ inches on all sides).
- Arrange your information in blocks under separate headings separated vertically from one another by blank space.
- Be consistent—handle similar parts of your résumé the same way throughout.

To achieve the format you want, you may have to type your résumé over many times. Do not get discouraged and settle for a sloppy, inaccurate, inconsistent, or unattractive job. Remember, you are applying for a job as a *writer*. The people who hire writers are writers and editors themselves. They worry about inconsistencies, misspellings, and sloppiness because they do not want people who write or edit that way in their organizations.

**As an applicant for a writing job, you must be sure your résumé is absolutely letter-perfect. It must be well written. It must contain no spelling, grammatical, or typographical errors. To produce even one page of error-free material is quite a challenge, but you must meet that challenge or you will never see the inside of an employer's office.**

Once you get one good typing of your résumé prepared, do not try to reproduce it by typing it over and over again. Rather, get it printed or reproduced on a good office copier for future use.

When you send out your résumé (in answer to an advertisement, for example), it should be accompanied by a brief letter of transmittal that tells what ad you are responding to, that you are interested in the job, that your résumé is enclosed, and, perhaps, why you think you are especially well qualified for the job in question.

Remember: Your letter of transmittal must be letter-perfect, too!

*The Interview*

If your résumé strikes a responsive chord with a company, you will be invited to the company's plant for an interview. In the interval between receipt of the invitation and departure for the interview, learn as much as you can about the company. Go back to the booklets in the placement office. Check Standard & Poor's "Standard New York Stock Exchange Stock Reports" in the library. Look at their product advertising in popular and trade magazines. Try to get a feel for what sort of company it is, what it does, and what it makes. The more you learn beforehand, the more intelligent your questions can be during the interview.

The employment process varies considerably from company to company. Most organizations like to have you fill out their own employment application form. Some will send it in advance, some will ask you to fill it out when you arrive for the interview, some will let you take it along to fill out after the interview. Some companies will ask you to take one or more intelligence, aptitude, personality, or interest tests; others will not.

All, however, will have their staff members talk to you. This is "the interview." Usually you will talk first to a personnel representative who will expertly put you at ease, tell you something about the company, ask a bit about your background, and tell you who else you are to talk to. Then you will talk to one or more department heads for whom you might work. They will worry less about putting you at ease, but rather will get right to the business of finding out what you know, what kind of person you are, what your training and experience has been, and so on. They may ask to see samples of your work, and you should have some with you.

As a rule, they will also talk about what job they are trying to fill. If they do not, you must ask them, for it is *your* interview as well as theirs. You need to find out about the job and what it entails just as much as they need to find out about you.

Before you leave, you should also, probably from the personnel man, inquire about probable salary, working hours, housing, and such fringe benefits as life insurance, health insurance, retirement plans, profit sharing, stock options, vacation and sick leave, and any others that may be appropriate.

## A Time of Waiting

In rare cases, you may be offered a job at the time of the interview. Usually, however, an employer will be looking at several candidates, and it may take anywhere from two weeks to two months for him to decide whether to make you an offer.

During that period, you should be following up other leads, and, hopefully, having more interviews. You may need to have half a dozen interviews to get one job offer.

*What Salary Can You Expect?*
Here is a list of 1970 annual salaries for various types of technical and science writers and editors.

| | |
|---|---|
| Technical Manual Writer | $6,000 to $16,000 |
| Technical Report Writer | $8,000 to $20,000 |
| Newspaper Journalist | $6,000 to $16,000 |
| Science Writer | $8,000 to $20,000 |
| Magazine Editor | $8,000 to $25,000 |
| Free-Lance Writer | $5 to $25 per hour |
| Contract Agency Writer | $5 to $10 per hour |

Those figures are derived from occupational guides, association surveys, and personal communications. The first column of numbers represents approximate starting salaries for relatively inexperienced people. The second column represents mid-career or peak salaries for people who remain in that particular specialty until retirement.

By moving into supervision or by doing free-lance work, experienced people can increase the top figures by as much as another $10,000.

As Henry Goodman, of the Council for the Advancement of Science Writing, says:

Science writers believe they earn just a bit more than most other journalists with equal seniority and experience. Salaries range from (depending upon the size of the publication) about $8,000 annually up to $20,000, and there are many free-lance opportunities, so that a good science writer can earn $30,000 or more a year. A few free-lancers also make that much.

During the past ten to fifteen years salaries in those fields have been increasing at a rate of 4 to 5 percent each year. Beyond 1970, an increase of at least 3 percent per year can be expected.

*Getting a Job with the Federal Government*

As we have indicated, the federal government employs many writers and editors. In years past, government salaries tended to lag behind those in business and industry. Recent government salary increases have brought federal salaries to about the same level as those in business and industry. Government fringe benefits tend to be better, on the whole, than many industrial packages.

As we write, however, job openings in government are quite scarce, and the procedures for getting such jobs are more involved than are most industrial employment procedures.

First, you must establish your eligibility for employment by taking the Federal Service Entrance Examination. When your eligibility is established, your name is then placed on a waiting list for various types of job openings. When an agency has an opening, it reviews the eligible candidates and selects those it wishes to interview. At present, this procedure can result in very long delays between establishing eligibility and receiving your first call for an interview.

The U.S. Civil Service Commission publishes four guidance booklets that tell pretty much the whole story:

> "Go Government," BRE-14
> "Working for the U.S.A.," Pamphlet 4
> "Federal Service Entrance Examinations,"
>     Announcement No. 410
> "Federal Career Directory, A Guide for College Students."
>     Supt. of Documents,
>     U.S. Government Printing Office,
>     Washington, D.C. 20402. $1.25.

Except for the Directory, the booklets may be obtained at no charge from the U.S. Civil Service Commission, 1900 E Street, N.W., Washington, D.C. 20415. They may also be available at your local library or your nearest Civil Service office.

(Don't overlook writer opportunities with state and local governments.)

*Now You're on the Job*

You have received an offer, and have accepted it.

The intensive learning starts now; what went before in school was only general. Now you will clearly see distinct goals in terms of money and achievement, and the things you must do to achieve those goals will be apparent.

Most important: Give full value. Not only will you advance, but you will also create a record of accomplishment that will open the door to many new opportunities.

# CHAPTER X

## Groups That Can Help You

"Americans are the greatest of joiners," it has been said, and American writers in the fields of science and technology are no exception. Writing is essentially a solitary activity, and to relieve the loneliness of that solitude, writers like to get together in professional associations to trade information, to discuss their problems, and to learn from one another.

A newcomer to the profession can be helped greatly by joining a group in his field of interest. This chapter describes two types of association that can be of benefit to the writer: those specifically for writers and those concerned primarily with science or engineering. Many writers join both types to get maximum benefit from associations.

Associations take a special interest in the newcomers to their profession, recognizing the fact that they will be the members who will take the place of the present membership in times to come. Most of them provide student memberships and associate memberships that provide most of the advantages of full membership at reduced cost. The reduction extends to attendance fees at conventions and seminars, and to all other benefits the association can offer. As the newcomer gains in experience (and income), he advances in grade to the highest level he can attain.

Selecting an association is a matter of matching your interest to the right group. All of them provide descriptive literature (see Fig. 13) at no cost, and those with a chapter in your vicinity will recommend a member whom you can contact for further information, and who will perhaps invite you to be his guest at a meeting. Many association chapter meetings are open to anyone interested in attending.

*Fig. 13. Descriptive literature is available from most professional associations
on request.*

## Groups of Interest to Writers

### American Medical Writers Association (AMWA)

AMWA is the largest association dedicated to the advancement
and improvement of medical communication. Its membership includes medical editors, writers, publishers, illustrators, and science
writers on biomedical subjects for radio, television, and other mass
media.

AMWA provides courses and workshops for guidance in the art
and techniques of medical communication.

The association holds a national convention each year. AMWA's
major publication is the *AMWA Newsletter,* which is issued bimonthly. Its topics include advice about medical writing, news of
members and chapters, and employment information.

If you are a full-time student, you may apply for *Student Membership.* Otherwise you should apply for *Active* or *Life Membership.*

### Association of Petroleum Writers (APW)

APW is a national professional society made up of writers in the petroleum field who prepare material for the trade and daily press. Its objectives are the improvement of proficiency and standards in the field of journalism and a broader understanding of the techniques of dealing with petroleum topics.

Publications include a six-times-yearly *APW Bulletin* and a roster of the membership. A national meeting is held each year.

Full-time participants in petroleum writing may be full *Members.* Those who are in related activities, such as public relations, may be *Associate Members.*

### Aviation/Space Writers Association (AWA)

Members of this association tell the story of general and commercial flying, of air power, and of the attempts to conquer space. Their objective is to maintain high standards of quality and veracity in gathering, writing, and disseminating information.

The membership comprises aviation/space writers and editors of newspapers, magazines, books, radio, television, and press services in all parts of the United States and Canada. Public relations representatives, public information officers, and writers employed in industry and by the government are admitted as associate members.

Services that members receive include professional accrediting, opportunities for press tours (see Fig. 14) and field trips, and recognition as professionals. The association sponsors several awards for excellence in writing, and for outstanding service to the profession of aviation and space writing. There are periodic regional meetings, and one national news conference and meeting held each year.

Publications include the *Newsletter* for the members, and the *AWA Manual,* an informative guide for writers. *Ink and Avgas* is the twenty-fifth anniversary publication that tells the history of the association from 1938 to 1963.

There are two primary classes of membership: *Members,* who are active in aviation and space writing and whose work appears in the public media; and *Associate Members.* There is also a *Student Mem-*

Fig. 14. AWA members inspect the XB-70 at Wright-Patterson Air Force Base during the 31st annual news conference and meeting.

PHOTO BY DAVE LUTES (AWA) OF DAYTON, OHIO

*ber* category for those who are studying journalism with the aim of becoming aerospace writers.

### National Association of Science Writers (NASW)

Members of NASW inform the public about all kinds of science through all kinds of media: They report rocket shots in newspapers, produce television shows about surgery, and prepare magazine articles and books on every field from astronomy to zoology. Other members report science indirectly through special publications other than the news media.

A primary objective of the association is to strengthen the link between scientists and the public. It also works to remove unnecessary restrictions on news dissemination.

Two major meetings are held annually: one in June with the American Medical Association, the other in December with the American Association for the Advancement of Science.

A quarterly publication, the *Newsletter,* tells what is happening in the field. Another quarterly, the *Clipsheet,* reprints science stories by members.

There are two major classes of membership: *Active* and *Associate.* Active members write science news for the public. Associate members are public information officers who write science news for hospitals, government agencies, universities, and similar organizations.

### Public Relations Society of America (PRSA)

PRSA is an association of public relations people employed by industry, consulting firms, government, and trade and professional associations. They are the point of contact between their employers and the general public. Their media of communication are radio and television, newspapers and magazines, and special publications such as company annual reports. If their organizations are active in science and technology, they describe and interpret such activities for the public.

Services of the society include professional accreditation (for the grade of *Member*), and local, regional, and national meetings. There are two major publications: the *Public Relations Journal,* and the *Public Relations Register.*

Membership is in three grades: *Accredited, Associate,* and *Pre-*

*Associate.* There is also an auxiliary group for students of public relations—the *Public Relations Student Society of America.*

### Society for Technical Communication (STC)

STC is the largest professional organization dedicated to the advancement of technical communication in all media. Its membership includes technical writers and editors, illustrators, advertising copywriters, educators, engineers, audio-visual specialists, librarians, and many others. Before July 1971, it was called the Society of Technical Writers and Publishers.

There are fifty chapters in the United States and Canada. STC conducts an international conference each year. Society chapters sponsor periodic seminars, symposia, and special training courses. The society conducts art and publications competitions and exhibits. It gives awards and other recognition for outstanding performance by its members.

The society publishes a bimonthly journal, *Technical Communication,* that covers a broad range of topics of interest to writers and illustrators. It issues bibliographies and standards, and publishes a national newsletter. Most chapters publish their own local newsletters.

There are four applicative grades of membership: *Senior Member, Member, Associate Member,* and *Student Member.*

### Other Groups of Value to Writers

In addition to those groups specifically organized for writers, there are many others of value in the subject-matter field of the writer; that is, in science or engineering. Many of the groups recognize the importance of writers and writing, and have established special sections for them. Such groups are invaluable in keeping one's knowledge up-to-date.

### American Association for the Advancement of Science (AAAS)

AAAS is not only the largest federation of scientific organizations, but it also has more than 130,000 individual members. Its objective is to further and facilitate the work of scientists and to increase public understanding and support of the efforts of scientists.

Its publications include the widely known weekly journal, *Science,* the *AAAS Bulletin,* and several other publications designed to enhance science and scientific communication.

Its national conference is held in December. It also holds divisional meetings, special seminars, and symposia. Prizes and awards are given for outstanding contributions to science and to science writing.

The AAAS has a special group for writers called the *Section on Information and Communication,* and the *National Association of Science Writers* holds its winter conference with the AAAS national meeting in December.

There is one grade of membership, and no restriction on membership except that one must be a scientist or have an interest in science.

## American Society of Mechanical Engineers (*ASME*)

ASME is a society of more than 60,000 members, of which 9,000 are student members. The primary purposes of the ASME are to disseminate information, develop standards and safety codes, and encourage personal and professional development.

*Mechanical Engineering* is the society's primary publication. There are also seven other journals covering topics such as power and lubrication. The ASME publishes codes and standards, handbooks, and proceedings and symposia volumes.

National meetings and conferences are held annually. Local section meetings provide opportunities for personal contact with other members.

There are five grades of membership: *Member, Associate Member,* two affiliate memberships, and *Student Member.*

## Institute of Electrical and Electronics Engineers (*IEEE*)

IEEE is the world's largest engineering society. The requirement for membership is an interest in electrical or electronics engineering.

There are thirty-one separate sub-groups available to the membership, each of which covers a special interest within the field. For example, Group G-4, *Circuit Theory,* and Group G-26, *Engineering Writing and Speech.* The latter group has these purposes:

The study, development, improvement, and promotion of the techniques for preparing, organizing for use, processing, editing, collecting, conserving, and disseminating any form of information in the electrical and electronics field.

Each of the groups has its own publication called the *Transactions*. The monthly *Spectrum* contains articles of interest to the whole membership, and is available to all members.

The IEEE sponsors the country's largest technical meeting, which is held in New York City every March. Local chapter and regional meetings are conducted periodically.

Four membership grades are offered: *Senior Member, Member, Associate Member,* and *Student Member*. A special publication is offered to students: the *IEEE Student Journal*.

There are many more groups of interest to writers. Additional lists are provided in Appendix B, together with information on how to find out more about all of them.

*To Summarize*

Professional associations can do these things for you:

- Provide up-to-date information about new techniques, new equipment, new opportunities—in short, information about how to become more effective in your profession.
- Provide job leads both through advertisements and through personal contacts.
- Offer valuable trade news: data on new products, ads for contract services, ads for equipment, and so on.
- Assist in continuing education by sponsoring informative seminars and symposia.
- Provide opportunities for social contact between those with similar professional interests.
- Conduct research to determine the effectiveness of the profession in meeting its objectives.
- Advise educational institutions on curricula for the education of technical and science writers.
- Work with regulatory agencies to remove restrictions that may hamper the work of writers.
- Provide for accreditation and other recognition of one's professional standing.

- Establish and maintain liaison with allied groups, and sponsor joint meetings for mutual benefit.
- Provide incentive for the betterment of the profession by means of awards and other recognition for outstanding achievements.

Valuable? Indeed!

# CHAPTER XI

# Where Can You Go from Here?

Where will the career of technical and science writing take you? What does the future hold? Will the career be a meaningful one —will it bring not only an adequate monetary reward, but also satisfaction and fulfillment?

This chapter offers a prediction of the role that technical and science writers will play during the span of your working career—the time between now, the decade of the 1970's, and the decade of 2000–2010 A.D.

This span of time will be an exciting one, since when the bimillennium comes on December 31, 1999, the men of the present will seem as antiquated as the men of the 1700's do to us now.

There will be many wonders: controlled climate under plastic domes over population centers, automated medical exams with computer diagnosis, freedom from most diseases, thermonuclear power sources. The writer will play a role in all of them.

## Your Role in the New Communication

For thousands of years, men have communicated and recorded knowledge by the process of writing words and drawing pictures and symbols by hand, first on stone, then on lighter and more portable materials such as papyrus and parchment. Knowledge so recorded was accessible only to a very few, since copies could be made only by hand, tediously and expensively.

Then Gutenberg invented movable metal type. Recorded knowledge became widely available, and men apart could communicate with one another. The result was a cross-fertilization of ideas and a growth of new knowledge that has culminated in what is now called "the information explosion."

Now a new process of communicating and recording knowledge has come into existence—a process that is perhaps even more revolutionary and far-reaching in its effects than the invention of Gutenberg. It is the processing of information by electronic means. It provides a storehouse of infinite capacity, and lightning-speed retrieval and display. Call it the *New Communication*.

But right now, in the decade of the 1970's, we are at about the same stage of development of the process as was Gutenberg when he assembled his first experimental type characters into a word. We are now faced with an incredible amount of miscellaneous hardware and techniques for using it—audio and visual tape recorders, television and special displays, photo-image storage systems and readouts, film projectors, teaching machines, holographic devices, and, most important, the computer.

All of them have yet to be combined into an effective whole. The promise of what can be done was first shown in EXPO '67 in Montreal, where exciting "multi-media" displays were shown.

The promise of the process is incredible, but the promise must be brought to fulfillment. Technical and science writers will play a key role in making it possible; in so doing, they will be pioneers in developing systems for educating and training and communicating that will change society profoundly within their lifetimes.

\*     \*     \*

The time will come when you will sit before a display console, and summon up instantaneously any part of the entire range of all recorded knowledge. Freed from the tedium and uncertainty of searching through libraries, your full powers of reasoning and creativity can be brought to bear upon the problem.

\*     \*     \*

## You May Be an Educator

Mankind's future, whether it be good or ill, depends to a large measure on the effectiveness of its educational system. Here again, the surface has only been scratched as to what can be done. In the hands of the Education Writer, the *New Communication* will revolutionize the education process. Learning will not be so much a matter of reading about and hearing about a topic, and learning by rote, but of *experiencing*.

Let us say the topic of study is Ancient Rome:

> . . . you will step into a chamber whose invisible walls can be contracted close about you, or expanded to infinite size, as the need requires. About you will suddenly appear a street in Rome, with its people, its sights, its smells, the sound of the Latin tongue and the clatter of carts—all the color and life of that ancient time. You will walk as one invisible among them, experiencing life as it was then. As you turn a corner, you may come upon the soothsayer calling his warning to Caesar . . .
>
> It will be as if you were there.

Then education will be as it basically is, and should be—high adventure!

*You Can Rebuild the Reputation of Science*

Since the first atomic blast, the reputation of science has deteriorated to the point that much of the world's trouble and tumult is being laid at its doorstep. And there is a measure of truth in the indictments, as too many of the discoveries have been used to make war more horrible and the earth less livable. The forces that science has released, once locked tightly in the earth and in the universe, threaten to destroy all life within a generation. Yet science of itself is not to blame—indeed only through further use of science have we any hope of rehabilitating our environment.

As a technical and science writer, your most important function may well be to rebuild the reputation of science—a necessary step in ensuring the support of science by all sectors of society. Without that support, progress could come to an end.

But along with that rebuilding there must be influence to guide men and society in the sane and proper use of the forces that have been unlocked.

The writer can be that influence. His words can change the world.

*Your Words Can Change the World*

> For each of us, as for the robin in Michigan or the salmon in the Miramichi, this is a problem of ecology, of interrelationships, of interdependence. We poison the caddis flies in a stream and the salmon runs dwindle and die. We poison the gnats in a lake and the poison travels from link to link of the food chain and soon the birds of the lake margins become its victims. We spray our elms, and the following spring, springs are silent of robin song, not because we sprayed the robins directly but because the poison traveled, step by step, through the now familiar elm leaf-earth-worm-robin cycle. These are matters of record, observable, part of the visible world around us. They reflect the web of life—or death—that scientists know as ecology.[1]

So wrote science writer Rachel Carson in *Silent Spring,* the first effective cry against the indiscriminate poisoning of our life-space by pesticides and defoliants. And her first cry was followed by an ever growing chorus of protest raised against pollution of all kinds.

She wrote another thing, did Miss Carson—pertinent now, and in the times to come.

> We live in a time when it is easy to despair, but it is also a time of great hope. We live in a time when it is necessary to know for what we stand, and to take that stand with courage.[2]

*You May Write to Entertain*

The average number of hours individuals work each year in the early 1970's is about 2,000. By 2000 A.D., that number will be cut in half, giving each worker an additional 1,000 hours of free time.

How will that time be spent?—surely not in watching an endless round of sporting events, or interminable soap operas.

There will be some of that, of course, but such fare will not be accepted as a steady diet. There will be great demand for a higher quality of entertainment—entertainment that utilizes all the techniques

---

[1] Rachel Carson, *Silent Spring* (Boston: Houghton Mifflin Company, 1958).
[2] *Audubon Magazine,* October 1963.

of the *New Communication*. Again, as for education, the one entertained will be almost a participant, not only hearing and seeing, but *experiencing*.

A fit topic for much of that entertainment will be science and technology. Like the poet who can perceive an infinity of wonders in what others view as the commonplace, so can the science writer draw upon a storehouse of marvels with which to entertain. At the same time, he will educate and influence the lives of men to come in good ways.

\*  \*  \*

The time will come when you will be able to communicate face-to-face with any person, or any group, in any part of the world, not as a picture and a sound, but as if you were there in the flesh before them, and they before you.

\*  \*  \*

### The Ten Great Tasks

It is said that these will be the areas of foremost achievement during the next 100 years:[3]

1. Transportation
2. New energy and power sources
3. Conservation and pollution control
4. Biomedical engineering
5. Communications
6. General new products and materials
7. Space technology
8. Oceanology
9. Urban and remote area development
10. Food production and distribution

Hitch your wagon to one of them, for technical and science writers will play a key role in making those achievements possible.

At the close of his career in the Eighteenth Century, Sir Isaac Newton said this:

---

[3] From a study by Keuffel & Esser Company. Press release, October 22, 1968.

I seem to have been only like a boy playing on the seashore, and diverting myself in now and then finding a smoother pebble or a prettier shell . . . , whilst the great ocean of truth lay all undiscovered before me.

We seem to have come a long way in the two-hundred-odd years since Newton, but in reality, we have found only a few more pebbles and shells, and the great ocean still lies undiscovered before us.

*There Will Always Be a Writer*
Behind every communication, there will always be a writer. For every new discovery in science, and for every new development in technology, there must be a report and an interpretation and assessment of its impact upon society. For every new device, there must be instructions for its operation and maintenance, and a listing of its components. For every selling message, every advertisement, every entertainment, there will always be a writer to arrange the information into a form acceptable to the audience, and to adapt it to the medium of communication.

The name *writer* may change as the emphasis shifts from the printed word to the *New Communication*. But call him what you will, there will always be the one who builds the bridges of communication between men and groups and nations.

\*          \*          \*

*A Closing Word*
This is in all likelihood a time of uncertainty for you, and perhaps more than a little anxiety. You must make a decision that may prove to be the most important of all in your lifetime—the choice of a career.

But there will come a day when the years have softened the urgency of this moment, a day when you will look back upon this time as the start of a great adventure—*your* adventure—because you are unique in this world—no one like you has ever existed, nor have the circumstances ever been the same. Hence the path you will follow is uncharted. Your great adventure will be in going down that path, which is unique and yours alone.

If you can recognize the adventure of it now, rather than several years hence, this time of now will take on a special meaning that will relieve the anxiety and make it the exciting fun it is.

Whatever career you choose, may good fortune go with you.

*Emerson Clarke*

*Vernon Root*

# Typical Sources of Education

In this Appendix, five typical courses of study are described, three of which are offered by colleges.

The courses are:

- Technical journalism program
- Medical writing program
- College extension short course
- Company-sponsored course in writing
- Seminar sponsored by an association

## Technical Journalism Program

The following description is excerpted from *Professional Careers in Technical Journalism,* a brochure issued by the Technical Journalism Division of Colorado State University, Fort Collins, Colorado.

Progress in science is dependent upon skilled communications. The technical journalist's job is to interpret the results of research in such fields as atomic energy, electronics, medicine, chemistry, agriculture, physics, and psychology, in terms that are interesting and meaningful.

The four-year program at Colorado State leads to a Bachelor of Arts degree.

The student selects a minor area of concentration in which he takes at least thirty hours of credit. This option might be general science and technology, or the physical, biological, or social sciences.

The student may also combine his interest in technical journalism with his major in forestry and range management, engineering, veterinary medicine, industrial arts, industrial construction, management, business, or speech.

*Courses You May Take*

The program of courses to prepare the students for the profession includes:

Introduction to Mass Communications
Basic News Writing
News Editing
Interpretive News Writing
Advertising Copy and Layout
Basic Photography
Applied Photography
Basic Business Communications
History and Principles of Journalism
Beginning Magazine Article Writing
Writing the Scientific and Professional Article
Agricultural Journalism
Basic Technical Writing
Television News Documentaries
Advanced Technical Writing

Business and Industrial Publications
Writing in Public Relations
Advanced Writing in Public Relations
Communications Law
Commercial Motion Picture Script Writing
Graphics for the Technical Editor
Ethics and Journalism
Technical Literature
Radio and TV News Writing
Communicating Change
Process of Mass Communications
Technical Editing
Radio-Television News
Communications Research Methods

*Medical Writing Program*

Joye Patterson, Assistant Professor of Journalism of the University of Missouri at Columbia, describes the medical writing program as follows:

At Missouri, undergraduates in the School of Journalism may indicate medical writing as an area of concentration. To do so, they must complete at least 21 hours in the sciences, and take certain specified journalism courses (including reporting, features, and science writing).

The science courses may be selected on the basis of the student's particular scholastic background and his career interests. For example, he may (1) take introductory courses in a number of science areas (e.g., chemistry, zoology, ecology, psychology, etc.) in order to acquaint him with basic concepts and terminology and to form the basis for perhaps further study in one or more of these areas. Or (2) he may spend a fifth year and receive both Bachelor of Journalism and Bachelor of Science degrees.

The program in medical writing is open also to graduate students. Many of these students enter the School of Journalism with an undergraduate degree in one of the sciences.

The University also offers two off-campus programs to graduate students, which enable students to gain practical experience in medical writing under the supervision of experienced newsmen.

*The College Extension Short Course*

The short course provides intensive instruction in a new technology, or (in the example that follows) instruction in technical writing and editing.

This five-day course was developed and taught by Professor John B. Bennett of Harvard University and Professor Robert R. Rathbone of MIT. Many guest lecturers from colleges and industry have been called upon. The course has been presented at UCLA every summer since 1963, with Professor Craig B. Smith as course adviser.

It will be noted that time is allotted for maximum student involvement.

*First Day:*  The writer's role/The reader's needs
Introduction
Principles of good writing
The writer and his responsibilities
Individual conferences
The editor and his responsibilities
The writer at work (instructor and student panel)

*Second Day:*  Effective style/The editor's role
Effective style

Publications management (instructor and student panel)
Individual conferences
The editor and his responsibilities
The editor at work
Lecture (topics chosen by participants)

*Third Day:* How to edit/Word choice and usage
The process of editing
The role of graphics
Individual conferences
Word choice and usage
Books for the writer
Lecture (topics chosen by participants)

*Fourth Day:* Special problems/Oral presentations
Self-improvement
Technical proposals (guest lecturer and student panel)
Individual conferences
Analysis of assigned reading
Oral presentations: the writer-editor's role
Lecture (topics chosen by participants)

*Fifth Day:* Production methods
Office composition (demonstration)
Individual conferences

## Company-Sponsored Course in Writing

Perceiving a lack of writing skill among those who are required to write in the course of their work, many companies have set up in-plant training courses. An excellent example is the twelve-week, forty-eight-hour intensive course in writing developed by Max Weber, Senior Technical Editor, for Argonne National Laboratories. Here is his outline:

1. The process of writing
   A. Defining subject
   B. Assembling material
   C. Making outline
   D. Writing to outline
   E. Rewriting

2. The fundamentals of writing
   A. Words as units of meaning
   B. Words in groups
3. Common writing problems
   A. Analysis of word order
   B. Other problems: Pronoun reference, passive voice, parallelism, etc.
4. Punctuation
   A. Review of punctuation marks
   B. Application
5. Diction
   A. Choosing words and phrases for proper meaning
   B. Eliminating "deadwood" and clichés
   C. Verb mutilation
   D. Vocabulary building
6. Style
   A. Developing a style
   B. Adapting to a set space
   C. Proper position for emphasis
   D. Relationship of ideas

The practicality of the course is enhanced by techniques such as class analysis of student writings, and alternating the writing class with a complementary course in effective speaking. (Excerpted from a paper presented by Max Weber at the Seventeenth International Technical Communications Conference sponsored by the Society of Technical Writers and Publishers.*)

*Seminar Sponsored by an Association*
Associations often sponsor special meetings to keep their membership up-to-date on the latest developments. Here is an example—a one-day seminar offered by the Boston Chapter of the Society of Technical Writers and Publishers* in 1970. Note that the speakers represent a cross section of industry, government, and academia, and that they are of a level that can speak with authority.

(The following is an excerpt from the brochure that advertised the seminar.)

---

* Now the Society for Technical Communication

(Title)    THE END OF COMMUNICATING: THE IMPACT OF
           TECHNOLOGY

A significant assessment is made of the state-of-the-art of
computer application to the documentation media. Presented
is a unique capsule exposé of new technological advances of
vital interest to an almost endless chain of professionals.

(Program)

| | |
|---|---|
| 8:00–8:30 | Registration |
| 8:30–8:45 | Introduction & Welcome |
| 8:45–9:30 | Richard Anné |
| | Vice President |
| | Manager of Computer Systems |
| | Volt Information Sciences |
| Subject: | "Computerized Data Systems" |
| | (Storage and Retrieval) |
| 9:30–10:15 | Gerald Vragel |
| | Manager, Systems Development |
| | Radio Corporation of America |
| Subject: | "Electronic Composition" |
| 10:30–11:15 | H. Lee Shimberg |
| | Chief of Publications Division |
| | U.S. Naval Ordnance Laboratory |
| Subject: | "Systems Configurations" |
| 11:15–12:00 | Dr. Coleman Bender |
| | Emerson College |
| Subject: | "Multi-Media Packages" |
| 12:00–1:45 | David B. Dobson, Keynote Speaker |
| (Lunch) | Publications Administrator |
| | Radio Corporation of America |
| Subject: | "The Automation Impact on Publications" |
| 1:45–2:15 | Henry Kerr |
| | Director of Programming |
| | ADAGE |
| Subject: | "Programmed Editing" |
| | (Film Presentation) |
| 2:15–2:45 | Dr. Beryl Payne |

School of Public Communications
Boston University
Subject:    "Information Overload! What to do about it!"
2:45–3:15   Harold Buchbinder
Chairman of the Board and
Chief Executive Officer
Benwill Publishing Corp.
Subject:    "Technology Transition in Publications"
3:30–4:30   Special Applications Panel
Robert Belote
Chairman, Air Force Publications
Specifications Study Group
Warner Robbins Air Force Base

Frank Winship
Mgr. Engineering Support Data
McDonnell/Douglas Aircraft Co.
"Weapons Systems Maintenance Action Center"

Frank Luttrell
Manager
NHA Data Tex
"Automation in the Storage and Retrieval of
    Technical Manual Information"
4:30–5:00   Question and Answer Panel
Queries will be solicited and answered
individually or collectively as fits the
situation. Most speakers are prepared to
remain until all matters raised to question
are brought to a conclusion.

# More About Associations

This Appendix lists the addresses of the associations described in Chapter X, provides a general list of other associations of interest to writers, and lists the three major sources of further information.

*Addresses of Groups Described in Chapter X*
American Medical Writers Association (AMWA)
420 Lexington Avenue
Suite 417
New York, N.Y. 10017

Association of Petroleum Writers (APW)
2659 South Quebec
Tulsa, Oklahoma 74114

Aviation/Space Writers Association (AWA)
101 Greenwood Avenue
Jenkintown, Pennsylvania 19046

National Association of Science Writers, Inc. (NASW)
P.O. Box H
Sea Cliff, New York 11579

Public Relations Society of America (PRSA)
845 Third Avenue
New York, N.Y. 10022

Society for Technical Communication (STC)
1010 Vermont Avenue, N.W.

Suite 421
Washington, D.C. 20005

*        *        *

American Association for the Advancement of Science (AAAS)
1515 Massachusetts Avenue, N.W.
Washington, D.C. 20005

American Society of Mechanical Engineers (ASME)
United Engineering Center
345 East 47th Street
New York, N.Y. 10017

Institute of Electrical and Electronics Engineers (IEEE)
345 East 47th Street
New York, N.Y. 10017

*Other  Associations*

The following are lists of associations of interest to technical and science writers; also listed are associations of those who support writers and work with them, such as illustrators, photographers, and printers. Addresses and further information about each can be found in the source books listed at the close of this Appendix.

*Other  Associations  for  Writers  and  Editors*

American Business Communication Association
Professor Francis W. Weeks, Executive Director
University of Illinois
Urbana, Illinois 61801

American Society of Business Press Editors
P.O. Box 34236
Washington, D.C. 20034

American Society of Magazine Editors
575 Lexington Avenue
New York, N.Y. 10022

Associated Business Writers of America
Hazel Palmer, Executive Secretary

P.O. Box 135
Monmouth Junction, New Jersey 08852

The Armed Forces Writers League, Inc.
George Washington Station
Alexandria, Virginia 22305

Education Writers Association
Pauline Stephans, Administrative Assistant
P.O. Box 1289
Bloomington, Indiana 47401

International Association of Business Communicators
2108 Braewick Circle
Akron, Ohio, 44313

International Communication Association
Professor M. Z. Sincoff, Executive Secretary
Ohio University
Athens, Ohio 45701

National Writers Club
745 Sherman Street
Denver, Colorado 80203

*Other Engineering Associations*
American Association of Engineers
American Institute of Chemical Engineers
American Institute of Industrial Engineers
American Institute of Mining, Metallurgical and Petroleum
    Engineers
American Society for Engineering Education
American Society of Agricultural Engineers
American Society of Civil Engineers
American Society of Lubrication Engineers
American Society of Photogrammetry
Association of Consulting Chemists and Chemical Engineers
Consulting Engineers Council
National Society of Professional Engineers
Society of Aerospace Material and Process Engineers
Society of Automotive Engineers

Society of Petroleum Engineers
Society of Logistics Engineers

*Other Science Associations*

American Academy of Political and Social Science
American Association for Laboratory Animal Science
American Chemical Society
American Institute of Physics
American Mathematical Society
American Nuclear Society
American Psychological Association
American Society for Information Science
American Society of Biological Chemists
Health Physics Society
Manufacturing Chemists Association
National Association for Research in Science Teaching
Society of Engineering Science
Society for Information Display
Soil Science Society of America

*Associations of Illustrators*

Association of Medical Illustrators
The Association of Professional Artists
The Association of Technical Artists
The National Association of Industrial Artists
Technical Illustrators Management Association

*Associations of Photographers*

Biological Photographic Association
Industrial Photographers Association of America
National Free Lance Photographers Association
National Press Photographers Association
Society of Photographic Scientists and Engineers
Society of Photo-Technologists

*Associations of Printers*

Creative Printers of America, Inc.
Education Council of the Graphic Arts Industries

Gravure Technological Association
Society of Reproduction Engineers
Society of American Graphic Artists

*Audio-Visual Associations*
Industrial Audio-Visual Association
National Audio-Visual Association
National Visual Presentation Association

*Associations of Interest to Aerospace-Defense Writers*
Aerospace Industries Association of America, Inc.
Aerospace Medical Association
Air Force Association
American Ordnance Association
Armed Forces Communications and Electronics Association
Armed Forces Management Association
Defense Supply Association
National Security Industrial Association

*Sources of Information About Associations*
One or more of the following catalogs of associations are available in most libraries. They supply information as to address, meetings, publications, and number of members.

*National Trade and Professional Associations of the United States.* Published each year by Columbia Books, Room 300, 917 15th Street, N.W., Washington, D.C. 20005

*Encyclopedia of Associations.* Gale Research Company, 1400 Book Tower, Detroit, Michigan 48226

*Directory of Communication Organizations.* Council of Communication Societies, P.O. Box 1074, Silver Spring, Maryland 20910

# Bibliography

"Advice to Authors." American Medical Association, Scientific Publications Division, Chicago, 1968.

*California Occupational Guides.* Department of Employment, State of California, Sacramento, California.

Clarke, R. E. *A Guide to Aerospace-Defense Contracts.* Industrial Press, Inc., New York, 1970.

Clarke, E. *A Guide to Technical Literature Production.* TW Publishers, River Forest, Illinois, 1961.

————. *How to Prepare Effective Engineering Proposals.* TW Publishers, River Forest, Illinois, 1962.

"The End of Communicating: The Impact of Technology." Brochure for a seminar. Boston Chapter, Society of Technical Writers and Publishers, October 23, 1970.

*Engineering as a Career.* Westinghouse Defense Center, Baltimore, Maryland.

*Federal Career Directory: A Guide for College Students.* Government Printing Office, CS1.7/4:C18/969.

Gould, J. L. *Opportunities in Technical Writing.* Universal Publishing and Distributing Corporation, New York, 1964.

"Graduate Studies in Technical Writing and Communication." Brochure. Rensselaer Polytechnic Institute, Troy, New York.

King, L. and C. Roland. *Scientific Writing.* American Medical Association, Chicago, 1968.

Lytel, A. *Technical Writing as a Profession.* Cincinnati, Ohio, 1959.
*Occupational Outlook Quarterly.* Bureau of Labor Statistics, U.S. Department of Labor.

"Professional Careers in Technical Journalism." Brochure. Colorado State University, Fort Collins, Colorado.

Root, V. M. "Technical Publication Job Patterns and Knowledge Requirements," *Technical Communications,* Third Quarter, 1968.

"Short Courses at UCLA." Brochure. University Extension, University of California, Los Angeles, June–July 1970.

*Survey for STWP Membership Profile.* Society of Technical Writers and Publishers, 1970.

"Technical Writers," an Occupational Handbook. Department of Labor, 1966–67.

"Technical Writing as a Career." Society of Technical Writers and Publishers.

Walter, J. A. "Education for Technical Writers," *STWP Review,* January 1966.

"Why Not Be a Technical Writer?" Leaflet 47. "Careers for Women" series. U.S. Department of Labor.

# Index

T
11
.C54
1976